T0276237

WRITE
YOUR
STORY

WRITE YOUR STORY

A Simple Framework to Understand Yourself, Your Story, and Your Purpose in the World

ALLISON FALLON

Forefront
BOOKS

Write Your Story: A Simple Framework to Understand Yourself, Your Story, and Your Purpose in the World
Copyright © 2024 by Allison Fallon

All rights reserved. No part of this publication may be reproduced, stored in a retrieval system, or transmitted in any form by any means, electronic, mechanical, photocopy, recording, or otherwise, without the prior permission of the publisher, except as provided by USA copyright law.

No patent liability is assumed with respect to the use of the information contained herein. Although every precaution has been taken in the preparation of this book, the publisher and author assume no responsibility for errors or omissions. Neither is any liability assumed for damages resulting from the use of the information contained herein.

Published by StoryBrand Books, an imprint of Forefront Books, Nashville, Tennessee.
Distributed by Simon & Schuster.

Library of Congress Control Number: 2024902610

Print ISBN: 978-1-63763-259-8
E-book ISBN: 978-1-63763-260-4

Cover Design by George Stevens, G Sharp Design LLC
Interior Design by PerfecType, Nashville, TN

Printed in the United States of America

For Nella and Charlie and all the
beautiful stories you will share

CONTENTS

FOREWORD

By Donald Miller

Years ago, I met a psychologist who gave me some advice about choosing friends. She said this: Choose people who have a story to tell, rather than those who tell stories.

When I asked for more, she said plenty of charming people tell stories as a way of entertaining others, but those who know their own story, those who have a story to tell about the mistakes they've made, the pain they encountered, and how they overcame all of it in order to transform, those are the healthy ones, the ones you can really connect with.

I believe her perspective is true.

I'm convinced that those who analyze their life and see it as a story are more content. I don't know why, exactly, because I'm not a psychologist. But I'm definitely practiced at the art. What I mean is, I've spent an embarrassing number of hours writing down stories that have happened to me. Having written a number of memoirs now, I can say with confidence that writing down your story, as self-absorbed as it may seem, is a deciding factor in the building of a meaningful life.

When I first started writing the stories of my life, I did so because I wanted to be seen and heard. And because I wrote those stories, I was seen and heard. In fact, as I shared my story with the world, I felt as though I'd eaten a Thanksgiving meal of attention and appreciation. This, strangely, healed something in me and helped me see beyond myself. After all, it's hard to think about anything else when you are hungry, and being seen and heard is a terrific way to get emotionally and psychologically full.

From a place of fulness, I was able to see others from a less needy place. I was able to listen because so many others had listened to me. And more interestingly than that, I knew better who I was, which helped me connect with those I needed to connect with and create distance from those I didn't believe would be kind or helpful to me and my story.

My guess is that those of us who have taken time to write down our stories better understand ourselves. In order to write your story, for example, you have to process the mistakes you've made. When writing your story, you have to think about the people you've hurt, your regrets, and all the dumb decisions that got you in trouble. A story is only interesting if the teller is vulnerable, after all.

It's in chronicling their mistakes a person learns not to make them again. I believe it's also true that the more you deny about your life, the dumber you stay.

Chronicling your mistakes is only half the assignment, though. When you write your story, you also get to reflect on your strengths, on all the things you've gotten right in your life. You get to own your wins and know for a fact they are yours, that you've somehow contributed positively to the collection of stories walking around next to you.

If you've ever talked to a person who seems to have made the same mistakes over and over, you were likely speaking with a person who did not know their own story.

In *Write Your Story*, my dear friend Ally Fallon teaches us to write our story, not for publication, but as a tool to generate self-awareness. And her process works. You will write your story in five pages or less, and when you do so, it will amaze you. You will discover that you are quite human, quite given to stupidity, and that you are brilliant and kind and forgiving. Mostly, though, what you will discover is that you are interesting. You are very interesting.

For me, the biggest benefit of learning to write my story (or more accurately, *stories*) is that it's brought to life a sense of gratitude. So much of life is forgotten, but when you write your story, you see what has happened, and you remember it, and you learn from it.

No matter how painful your story, when you write it all down, you feel a sense of inclusion in this life, and you realize, quite humbly, you are a tiny subplot in a grand and terrifying narrative that is ever so painfully arching toward a redemptive resolution, a resolution to which you become eager to contribute.

If you want to enjoy more of your life from here on out, take the time to understand who you are and to frame how you show up in the world.

I believe that those who do not know their story do not take responsibility for their story. For you, this book will change all of that.

This is not a book about learning to tell charming stories. Rather, it's a book that will transform you into a person with a story to tell, a story about how you became who you are and how painful that was, but also how thoughtful it made you.

The world needs more people like that.

CHAPTER 1

Why Write Your Story?

You are fascinating. You might not know this to be true about yourself yet, but I do. I know it's true because I've spent the past decade of my life helping people just like you take stories from their lives and turn those stories into books. My work as a ghostwriter and a book coach requires that I listen deeply to others in order to understand the events that have taken place in their lives and to bring the most riveting of those details to the surface. I can tell you with absolutely certainty: your story is interesting. As long as you know how to tell it.

Take my friend Sara, who came within nine days of marrying a bona fide con man. That's not how she would have told the story. She would have said she broke off an engagement. She likely would have downplayed the significance of the experience. It was embarrassing, after all—not to mention traumatizing. It wasn't an anecdote she went around sharing at dinner parties. That is until one day, when she was asked by a friend of a friend to come talk about this part of her life on a podcast.

At first Sara resisted the idea. She wasn't sure the story would be interesting to anyone but her. She worried she'd be judged or even humiliated when she shared what had truly taken place. But it was a small podcast, just getting its start. How many people would realistically be listening? And to be honest, the idea of having someone to talk to about the whole ordeal sounded kind of nice.

So she went on the podcast and shared. As it turns out, Sara's story was interesting to more than just a few people. Try hundreds of thousands of them. In one season, the podcast that was "just getting its start" turned into an award-winning show, with a massive and committed listenership. (You can hear Sara's story on Season 1 of *Something Was Wrong*.) The stories we are most afraid to tell are usually the ones that are most relatable.

Your story doesn't have to be heard by thousands of people to make it interesting. Take my friend Jennifer, for example, who adopted twin baby girls at birth. The details of her adoption story are private, for both court-ordered reasons and personal ones. It's nothing she's going to share on a podcast or put in a book. But I can tell you with absolute certainty that there are two people who will want to read her story one day: her two little girls. Jennifer gets to decide not only *if* she tells the story but also *how* she tells it.

She gets the phenomenal honor and privilege of passing on the narrative. So do you.

Or how about Mary, a woman I met at the park? We were each pushing our kids on the swings one morning, and we struck up a conversation, mostly about toddler things. When I told her what I do for work, Mary said she had a story to tell but couldn't put her finger on exactly what it was. She'd suffered through a big, dramatic childhood, and people seemed to really appreciate when she told that story. But she desperately wanted to move on from that narrative.

I asked her what she would write about if she could write about anything she wanted. She told me she'd write about becoming a mother. And then she whispered to me the secret no one else yet knew (except her husband), which is that she was newly pregnant with her second child.

"Why not write *that* story?" I asked.

"It's not like I'm the first person in the world to become a parent," she said. "Nothing I shared would be revolutionary."

Then Mary told me what she does for work. She's a parent coach, which means she comes alongside parents and helps them manage their anxieties around behavior problems so they can respond to their children with confidence in all kinds of situations. I stared at her for a minute to see if she was seeing what I was seeing—but of course she wasn't. Of all the people you would want to write a story about what it's like to become a parent, don't you think a parent *coach* would be one of them?

Sometimes we downplay or dismiss the things that are most interesting about us because we simply don't see ourselves the way someone else would.

Take Caleb for example. When I first met him, he was itching to write a book but still wasn't sure what the book would be about. He thought maybe it would be something to do with mental wellness in leadership, a subject he was passionate about.

I happened to know Caleb had played in the NFL and had graduated from West Point, one of the most prestigious military academies in the US, also having played football there. When I asked him where this fit in the story, he dismissed it. His NFL career was a failure, he said. And he didn't want to talk about West Point. Despite being a four-year starter, it was a largely unpleasant season of his life. Besides, all his friends from school had gone to war, and he'd gone to play football? That wasn't a story he wanted to tell.

But that's not how I saw the story. I didn't think of Caleb as a "failed" NFL player who couldn't hack a career in the military. I thought of him as one of the bravest men I knew. Here was an NFL player with insane mental toughness, who was waving a flag for men everywhere. He was saying, essentially, what does it matter if you play in the NFL if you can't sit still without having a panic attack? Who cares what kind of honor you achieve if you can't look yourself in the mirror at the end of the day? The very part of

Caleb's story he was ashamed to share was the most interesting part.

You might ask yourself, *Well, what does it matter if my story is interesting? Aren't there more important things in life than being interesting?* Maybe. But "interesting" literally means to catch or hold your attention. Don't you want your life to catch your attention? If your life isn't interesting to other people, I suppose that's fine. But what if your life isn't interesting to *you*?

WRITE YOUR STORY

The idea for *Write Your Story* came to me at dinner one night. My husband and I were with our friends Donald Miller and his wife, Betsy. At the time, I'd been working in publishing for nearly a decade, and Don's career in the writing world doubled mine. By then he had written several books, most of which had spent weeks or months on the *New York Times* bestseller list.

I had spent most of my adult life helping people take stories from their lives and turn those stories into book ideas. My work as a ghostwriter and a book coach was born from a bizarre concoction of interests. I'm the daughter of a therapist, an empath, a writer, a trained teacher, and a voracious reader. From a young age, I was fascinated by two things: understanding what motivates people and unlocking the single thread in a story that makes it all make sense.

This set of skills translated nicely to a job where I was tasked with putting together pitches for publishers, turning a complicated set of life experiences into a memoir anyone would want to read, and, at times, convincing the author that their story really *was* worth telling, no matter how much they questioned it.

I'd also written a few books of my own—including a memoir about my divorce. The experience of putting my own story on paper had fundamentally changed me and transformed my life in unthinkable ways. The experience made me question whether it mattered if you *published* your story as long as you wrote it down.

"I'd write books for the rest of my life," I told Don and Betsy at dinner that night, "even if I never sold another copy. It's *that* life-changing to write your story."

"That's what you ought to be teaching people," Don said.

The idea hit me like a bolt of lightning. Where had this idea *been* my whole life? I loved the publishing side of my work. But the more I thought about it, the more I realized there wasn't a huge difference between the well-known business leaders who got big book contracts and Mary, the woman I met at the park. They all questioned their ability and ideas. They all felt like imposters. They all told me they were "bad at grammar" and "not a real writer." And one of the biggest clients I'd worked with in my career (who has been on the *NYT* bestseller list multiple times) admitted to me that he's never finished reading a single book.

Each of these writers had a story they couldn't help but share. Yet they all questioned if they deserved to share it.

You have a different set of circumstances from Mary or Caleb or Jennifer or any of the well-known authors I work with, but the fact that you're holding this book tells me you have the same urge. Your story seems to grip you. You may worry it's not meaningful enough, worthy enough, inspiring enough, or interesting enough to write it down. But for reasons you do not fully understand, you can't shake the urge that you're supposed to tell it.

WHAT YOU'RE DOING
WHEN YOU WRITE

The urge to write your story is an urge to organize and clarify what has happened—and is happening—to you. Events that take place in our lives can seem, as we're living them, random and chaotic. And in many ways, they *are*. Consider this chain of events:

- Your two-year-old wipes yogurt all over your only clean pair of dress pants as you walk out the door to a meeting.
- Some guy cuts you off on the freeway as you're headed to work.
- Your boss gives you a "look" when you come in ten minutes late.

- Your computer won't connect to the Internet, so you have to troubleshoot.
- You scroll your favorite online site for ten minutes to give your brain a break.
- You meet an old friend for lunch and have a nice time.

I could go on, but you get the drift. It can appear like there's no clear plot, no arc, no common thread holding everything together. The whole thing can feel pointless and random, as if it has no clear direction. That's because it *doesn't* have clear direction—until you give it clear direction by deciding what the story is about. You get to decide what it means and what common thread holds all the parts together.

When you take the events of your life and filter them through the Write Your Story framework, you begin to see themes that were not apparent before. You begin to see yourself and your life with much more clarity.

When you take the events of your life and filter them through the Write Your Story framework, you begin to see themes that were not apparent before. Patterns become evident. There's no getting around it. You begin to see yourself and your life with much more clarity. Writing your story is like putting on a pair of glasses and looking in a mirror. Suddenly you become more aware of features you couldn't see before! The process is deeply restorative and peaceful. Deep down, we all intuitively know our story has meaning and that we matter.

Maybe you worry that your story is too boring to put on paper. Or maybe it's the opposite. Perhaps you're drowning in grief or loss or shame or guilt and cannot see your way out. Maybe you have a sadness or a rage that makes no sense to you. Maybe you are confronting addiction or recovering from trauma or just trying to discover what you believe about life or the world or yourself. Maybe you've witnessed miracles, and you want to share those with others as a way to inspire hope.

You might find yourself asking questions like:

- What is the meaning of all this?
- What role did I play in the way events unfolded?
- How does the world work?
- Is there a God? Or where was God in all of this?
- What is true about me and about this set of circumstances?
- What responsibility do I have moving forward?
- What can I learn from what I've experienced?
- How can I grow beyond this story and find a new path forward?
- How can I use my experience to inspire others?

What if the answers to these very questions are inside your story? And what if you uncover those answers when you write your story down?

You might say to yourself, *Aren't there some things for which we will never know the meaning?* Maybe. But the problem with that logic is that you are creating meaning out of your life whether you intend to or not. Your brain's job is to make sense of even the most senseless set of circumstances as a way to guide and protect you. Even "Life has no meaning" is a meaning *you* constructed to help a chaotic life make sense.

Our need for meaning is so foundational that, if we are not actively creating meaning in our lives, we will unconsciously take on the meaning someone else makes for us. Many of us take on the meaning our parents make of our stories. Their disappointments become our disappointments. Their frustrations become our frustrations. Their aspirations become our aspirations. The narratives they make up about us live inside of our heads as if they were our own.

We do this often with our spouses or partners. We take on a story they tell about us—which, even under the best of circumstances, is not the whole truth.

Even the most loving and well-intentioned parents or spouses do not deserve to decide what your life is about. That story is yours to write. The narratives other people write about us are biased and flawed and often have powerful agendas attached.

Take advertising, for example, which puts you square inside of a narrative that serves a specific purpose: getting you to buy something. If you haven't already solidly constructed meaning inside your own story, you won't be

WHY WRITE YOUR STORY?

equipped to choose if someone else's narrative fits. It's the difference between seeing yourself in the mirror and having someone else describe you to yourself. One is simply more precise than the other.

A client of mine, whom I'll call Jeremy, lost his wife in a tragic accident. He was then scrutinized and blamed in the media. In the midst of unthinkable pressure from the outside—literally, CNN trying to tell the story for him— Jeremy had to decide how he wanted to tell the story for himself. Not to appease the media but to survive his own grief and to honor his late wife. And that's exactly what he did.

Again and again, Jeremy and I pored over the events that had taken place. What emerged was an absolutely gorgeous love story where no detail was wasted. Even the tragedy itself couldn't wipe out the beauty of their love, which continued even after she was gone. That is the story that will go down in history for Jeremy, for his late wife, and for their children who will only know their mother through the stories told about her. Let's put the pen in the right hands.

To write your story is an intentional way to make meaning of your life.

Meaning-making cannot be escaped. Your choice is to do it intentionally or haphazardly. You can either make meaning yourself or allow someone else to do it for you. To write your story is an intentional way to make meaning of your life.

Let me ask you a question: Have you written the meaning to your story, or have you taken on the meaning someone else has written for you? When you write your story, you get to decide what you want it to mean.

- Why did my mother die?
- Why won't my business grow?
- Why did I hurt that person?
- Why did my father leave?
- Why do I always run out of money?
- Why don't I have a better relationship with my kids?
- Why am I so sad all the time?
- Is there more than this?
- What is the purpose of my life?

Meaning directs our lives. If the meaning you choose to attach to your story is, "Life is random and chaotic," then life will seem random and chaotic. If the meaning you attach is, "The world is a beautiful place," then you'll find yourself awed by the beauty around you, even when difficulties arise. What I'm talking about here is not as simple as positive thinking. What I'm talking about is looking more deeply at the events of your life and deciding what you would like to make them all mean.

Your story is the filter through which you see all of your experiences. Why not take a closer look at that filter by writing your story down?

THE GIFT YOU GIVE YOURSELF
WHEN YOU WRITE

My friend Cam is an accomplished, articulate, gifted author who has published several books and has seen her work reach the bestseller lists more than once. After writing her most recent book, Cam admitted something to me.

"I still haven't written *the one*."

I asked her to explain what she meant by "the one," and she said there was still a story inside of her that she hadn't allowed herself to write yet. That story, she admitted, was something so personal and vulnerable that she wasn't sure she would ever have the courage to tell it. She wasn't sure that a publisher would take interest. She wasn't sure that her readers would either. She worried it wouldn't sell. But she couldn't shake the urge that she wanted—no, *needed*—to one day write it.

This is a common sentiment I hear from even accomplished authors. There is the story they are being asked by agents and publishers to write, and then there is the story that is *begging* to be written.

Cam and I worked together to get her story down on paper. I won't share the details with you here because it's her story to tell, and she hasn't decided how exactly she wants to share it yet. But I will say this, before that story ever sits on a shelf—and even if it never does—it gave Cam the gift that writing gives to all of us. It revealed Cam to herself.

What we crave as human beings is not recognition. What we crave is authentic self-expression. Authentic self-expression is something you can give *yourself* without ever publishing anything.

So, before you opt out of this process by giving one of the excuses aspiring writers often give me ("I'm not a real writer" or "No one would ever read this"), ask yourself what would change for you if you were allowed to express yourself fully and authentically. What might you learn about yourself? What might change about your life? How might people treat you differently? What new opportunities might open up for you?

These are the gifts that writing gives you.

These are the gifts available to anyone who is ready to take them.

THE LIFE-CHANGING POWER OF WRITING YOUR STORY

My friend Justin came to me for help writing the story of his business, which had doubled in revenue year over year for five years and seemed to be barreling forward at an undeniable pace. Obviously, something was working very well for Justin on the business front, but he hadn't had the time to stop and figure out what exactly that was.

Justin didn't have much extra time in his day to write. He had a wife, three children, and a team of about twenty-five employees. His days started at 5 a.m. and didn't end until around 9 p.m., after family time and wrapping up responsibilities from the workday. And yet, writing his story was nagging at him, in large part because he had some big decisions to make moving forward, and he wasn't 100 percent clear which direction to take.

Even when things are going *great* inside your story, a lack of understanding will create confusion and uncertainty that can derail the narrative.

I spent a whole day with Justin, mapping out his story from start to finish, and we were able to pinpoint several reasons for his dramatic business success. One was straight-up luck. He had literally been in the right place at the right time with the right idea. Another was Justin's inherent magnetism. He had a way of drawing people to himself and gathering them around an idea. And the third had to do with a principle he called the "do less" effect.

The "do less" effect was about doing less to accomplish more. It was about working smarter, not harder. It was about operating under the belief that success is trying to happen for you and you'd have to literally *get in the way* in order to stop it.

He would tell his team explicitly that they wouldn't be rewarded for long hours logged, that he'd never expect them to come in to work on a weekend, and that he wasn't micromanaging their workday. In fact, Justin was frequently quoted as saying, "Nobody gets brownie points for suffering." As a result, his employees had an incredible loyalty to him and to each other. The team seemed to operate from an intrinsic motivation rather than an extrinsic one.

Perhaps the most shocking thing about Justin is that his set of beliefs didn't seem all that radical to him. It was just the way he had operated for as long as he could remember. He believed he would be successful, and he *had* been, over and over again. Sure, he'd had failures, but it was almost like they had faded into the background of the much more interesting stories of his success.

Our stories matter because we matter.

Once Justin saw the connection between his belief in success and his experience of success in the real world, the way forward wasn't confusing to him anymore. In fact, many things became clear. One of which was this: he personally needed to do way less. Justin needed to follow his own advice. He'd gotten lost in his own story and had been overworking himself, forgetting the very principle that had brought him here in the first place.

Thankfully, his story brought him back to himself.

Our stories matter because we matter. Because our lives don't have *one* meaning—they have infinite meanings. We get to decide which meaning makes it all click.

Writing your story can give you:

- Clarity about who you are and what really matters
- Confidence to move forward with a big goal

- A point of connection to someone you love
- Better physical health
- More joy and lightness in your life
- The ability to express yourself freely
- Sturdier, happier relationships
- A sense of being "at home" in your own skin
- An interesting story to tell about yourself
- A feeling of connection to those you love
- More empathy and compassion
- Healing from past pain
- Peace of mind
- Freedom from an old way of being

I am going to help you choose a story from your life and turn that story into three to five pages of writing you can share with someone else.

When I say "share," I mean that you may choose to share your story with a therapist or a friend. Perhaps you share it with a sibling or a child. You may choose to share your story with your spouse or even just with yourself. No matter who you share it with, do not underestimate the power of being honest with yourself for the first time.

What you will find is that writing your story helps you become more interesting. When you write your story, you will become more interesting to the people around the dinner table, to your coworkers, to your spouse, your children, and your friends. Most importantly, though, you will become more interesting to yourself. Writing your story is about changing your identity. It's about changing how you see yourself, how you talk about yourself, and how you carry yourself.

The truth is, you are already interesting. You are endlessly fascinating, and through the course of this book, I am going to help you pull the elements out of your story to prove to you that it's true. When you put the events of your story in the right order and apply meaning to those events, other people can learn from and be inspired by you.

When you're done with your story, you might expand it into a memoir or another kind of book. Maybe you share your story as a TED Talk or on another stage. Perhaps you share it with a book club or on social media or with another type of group. Whatever "share" means for you, by the end of this process, if you follow the guidance I give you, you'll have something tangible you can feel proud to share.

You could ignore that small but powerful invitation that's pulling you to write your story. Or you could give in to this process. You could dive below the surface of the water to meet the fullness of yourself for perhaps the first time. You could read the examples, follow the prompts, write your story, and discover something you might not yet know about yourself: You've been remarkable all along!

CHAPTER 2

What Is a Story?

Over a decade ago when I was writing my first book, I refused to use an outline. I would hear other writers talk about the frameworks they were using to construct their books, and it rationally made sense to me, but the whole thing felt too formulaic. I wasn't writing a book report, I told myself. This wasn't a science project. This was my *life*. Surely life is too complicated and nuanced for a formula.

My biggest concern with using a framework was that it would minimize the complexities of life and suck the mystery right out of the writing process. There was a part of me who loved how complicated it felt to write my story, and in a way I felt like it *needed* to be chaotic so I could have an excuse for why it was taking so long.

I had signed a contract with a publisher to write the manuscript in six months, but I was not making much progress. I had quit my full-time job to work on this project, and I was single at the time with no children, so I had the most enormous amount of time a person could possibly have available. Yet I was not moving the needle on my writing project.

I would go to a coffee shop in the morning and wait for inspiration to strike. When it didn't—and it usually didn't—I would wander around the city like a sad, lost little puppy, hoping for my muse to show up. When it didn't—and it usually didn't—I would meander home and spend a few more hours staring blankly at my blinking cursor until it was dark enough to go to sleep. The next day I would wake up and repeat the process all over again.

I *did* eventually finish that manuscript . . . three years later.

I wish I could say it took me so long to write the book because the finished product was just *that* good. I wish I could say it was my magnum opus, a truly revelatory piece of art. Unfortunately, none of those things were true. The book took me so long for one big reason. I had the wrong view of a formula.

I worried that using a formula to write would block inspiration and limit my agency, when the truth is, it's the other way around. Using a formula opens up agency and inspiration. Especially for a new writer, like I was at the time, a formula gives a healthy starting place from which you can build something all your own.

There are writers out there who say they "write without a formula" or "write without an outline." These writers are, in my experience, so deeply in tune with the formulas that make stories work that they don't even know they're using them. They don't need to think about it anymore. It lives inside their bones.

In order to write your story, you will need to understand the formulas that make stories tick. You might find yourself feeling resistant to using a formula like I was all those years ago. If that's the case, consider that resistance to be the first unseen way writing your story works to unlock your life.

What is that friction all about? Is it possible your resistance to structure is less about your ideal to be original and more about a hidden need to stay stuck? A framework will provide you the clarity you need. The question is: Do you want it? Do you want to have clarity in order to move forward, or is it oddly more comforting to be confused?

THE SHAPE OF A STORY

Stories are incredibly formulaic. Stories have a shape to them that is predictable and familiar. That shape is called an *arc*, and if a story doesn't have this shape, it feels clunky or boring. Perhaps you've watched a movie or read a book where you just kind of . . . lost interest. It's probably because the writer didn't do a good enough job of defining the arc of the story.

Story formulas are, in some ways, intuitive to us. Meaning, you might tell stories with an arc rather effortlessly, without thinking about it. You might walk into work on a Monday morning and say something like, "You'll never believe what happened to me this weekend!" What you're doing with that statement is initiating a story arc. There's tension that needs to be resolved. A question that needs to be answered.

That's how stories operate. They begin with a tension or a question and end with a resolution or an answer.

Although parts of storytelling can be intuitive, understanding deeply how stories work takes practice. Story formulas can feel confining at first because of how truly predictable they are. It's like walking down a narrow hallway—there's only one "right" way to go. And yet the more comfortable we get with story formulas, the easier it becomes to write your story.

As it relates to a personal story, like the one you are writing, the arc of the story is built around the transformation of the main character (whom we will call the hero). The story begins with the hero looking one way and ends with the hero looking some other way. It's possible not every problem will be resolved and not every question will be answered in the story. But the main problem the hero is facing *does* need to be solved. Perhaps even more importantly, the hero needs to change in some significant way; otherwise the arc won't be present, and your story will read as boring.

You might say to yourself, "What does it matter if the story is boring?" And I'd remind you that the first and most important person you're telling this story to is you. If *you* think your story is boring, if you can't find the arc, if you don't experience enough tension or resolution, you'll read your life like a boring book where you just sort of check out—which is what a great many of us are doing.

When you find the arc that drives your story forward, suddenly you begin to see life as undeniably riveting.

When you find the arc that drives your story forward, suddenly you begin to see life as undeniably riveting. Things may not resolve the way you thought they were going to, but you don't need them to. What you need to keep your story interesting is a hero who is willing to change. For instance:

- A hero who is closed off and angry but loses a loved one and becomes compassionate and soft
- A hero who was arrogant and perfectionistic but receives a terrifying diagnosis and gets in touch with his own weakness (which is actually his true strength)
- A hero who lacks confidence but, after being pushed to her limit by a bully, learns to stand up for herself

One image that always helps me think about a hero's transformation is the before and after reveals on those cheesy (and fun) "total makeover" shows. It could be a show about making over a house or a person, it doesn't matter. For some reason, viewers (not me, of course!) will watch episode after episode to see if yet *another* beat-up dump of a home can be transformed into a sparkling living space.

There is a reason why makeover shows are satisfying to millions of viewers, some of whom prefer not to identify themselves. They appeal to the part of us who understands a story arc. A strong "before and after" is compelling. The more dramatic the transformation, the more interesting the story.

So, what is the arc to your story? How does the hero of the story change from the beginning to the end?

THE WRITE YOUR STORY FRAMEWORK

To help you answer the arc question for yourself and give shape to your story, I'm going to teach you the Write Your Story (WYS) framework. This eight-part framework is based on concepts I've learned from storytelling experts like screenwriter, the late Blake Snyder and my friend and colleague Donald Miller. I am certified in Don's StoryBrand marketing framework, have coached hundreds of executives at StoryBrand marketing workshops, and have even traveled around the country as part of Don's team, delivering keynotes to various brands. If you're familiar with Don's work, you'll recognize parts of it here.

Different from the StoryBrand framework, though, this eight-part formula is specifically tailored to help you make sense of a personal story, which operates slightly differently from a screenplay or a brand narrative. Personal stories are my specialty—in part because of my work as a ghostwriter and a book coach—and in part because of my own life experience.

Shortly after I started working with StoryBrand, my life took an unexpected left turn. I found myself filing for divorce, sorting through a financial disaster, and quite literally wondering how I was going to pay my mortgage at the end of the month. It was a profoundly confusing time in my life.

And still, for reasons that didn't make sense to me at the time, I would feel pulled each morning to drive to my local coffee shop and write about what was happening to me. This later became my second book, *Indestructible* (Morgan James, 2018). But at the time there was no rhyme or reason to what I was writing. No arc. Just a bunch of desperate and frustrated words spilling out onto the page.

I had more questions than answers, more problems than resolutions, and no sense of what this story might actually be about.

Slowly, I started to use what I was learning about story formulas to see if I could give my experience some shape. Not all the "rules" applied, but I used the ones that did.

I clearly defined my problem. I identified my guides. I thought endlessly about what would have to happen for the story to resolve.

That experience showed me something. The more shape I gave to my story, the more my life started to speak to me. Wisdom that had been buried under the confusion and chaos of my circumstances floated to the surface. I began hearing what I call the "narrator voice" come through in my writing. Just like a narrator in a movie or a book, that voice seemed to know things I didn't know. It was like a higher, wiser part of me saw where the story was going. It was, quite literally, narrating my experience.

> *The more shape I gave to my story, the more my life started to speak to me.*

After I wrote that book, I realized something: personal stories, like all stories, follow predictable patterns. And when we can lean into the structures of storytelling and use them to organize our life experiences, it opens us up to a wisdom that is beyond our understanding. I've seen this wisdom in my own story and in the stories of hundreds of folks I've guided through this process.

The Write Your Story framework looks like this:

1. **The Controlling Idea**: what your story is about
2. **The Opening Line**: the hook you use to grip a reader

3. **The Hero Who Wants Something**: the character who sets the narrative arc
4. **The One Big Problem**: the obstacle that builds tension
5. **The Guide**: the character who helps the hero
6. **The Struggle + Relief**: the "roller coaster" of the story
7. **The Hero's Transformation**: how the story resolves
8. **The Moral**: the meaning you make of the story

In my book *The Power of Writing It Down* (Zondervan, 2021), I share the neuroscience behind the reasons writing about your life is powerful, and I offer an invitation to start for anyone who wants to give it a try. I even share prompts you can use to journal through the events of your life as they take place. In this book, I want to assist you in taking your writing process a step further. I want to help you organize your experiences into a specific shape called a *narrative arc*.

When you choose to submit the chaotic and random details of your life to a tool like storytelling, you see things from a different vantage point. Suddenly, your vision becomes much clearer. You know what your story is about. You can see where the resolution is headed. It may not be what you thought you wanted, but it is probably what you know you need.

And while the formula itself isn't so mystical, what's truly inexplicable is what happens when you apply it to your story. Your life begins to speak.

MAKE MAGIC OUT OF THE MUNDANE

You might have an inherently fascinating story to tell. I once worked with a writer who was held hostage for twenty-four hours by her undiagnosed schizophrenic boyfriend. Her story reads like an episode of *Law & Order*. But if that's not your experience, you're not at a disadvantage. Even a seemingly ordinary life still holds magic inside.

I understand the feeling of an ordinary life. At the time I'm writing this, I have a one-year-old and a two-year-old at home. My two-year-old daughter is obsessed with *PAW Patrol* and walks around singing the theme song over and over until it's stuck in my head. Before I left the house this morning to write this chapter, my one-year-old son rubbed mashed bananas all over my coat. I cleaned up the mess as best I could with a baby wipe, but I'll need to take the coat to the dry cleaner's later.

Riveting, I know.

The shape of a story is not created from extravagant details. The shape of a story is created through conflict and resolution. Through passion and desire. Through wanting something you can't yet have. Through believing something must be possible but not being able to make it happen (yet).

That is me, writing this book. I believe it can be easy and fun to write your story, and I want to make that possible for as many people as I can. For whoever would like to give it a try. It's what keeps me glued here to my seat in this coffee shop, in the sea of other monotonous things that might occur around me. The buzz of the espresso machine. The meeting happening at the table next to me. The slime smeared down the right arm of my coat.

Right now, I'm singularly focused. I will finish writing this book before the year's end. That's the story I'm writing—both figuratively and literally, I suppose.

So take a minute and consider what story you might be writing.

- Where is the conflict in your life?
- What's keeping you up at night?
- What drives you crazy?
- What makes you furious?
- What's blocking you or getting in your way?
- What do you want that you don't (yet) have?

Maybe for you, it's obvious. Maybe there's a big incident that happened earlier in your life that you'd like to write about. Losing a parent. Adopting your kids. Meeting your spouse. Leaving a toxic relationship. Growing a company. Suffering abuse.

Or perhaps you're not as sure. You'd like to write an interesting story, but your life seems to be a little flat. *Who would the hero be?* you wonder as you sit at your computer screen for the fourth consecutive hour. *What is the conflict?*

Does it count that the coffee shop was out of my favorite kind of milk?

It is in this way that storytelling invites us to do far more than commit our life to paper. It guides us to ask the big questions that stories answer.

Storytelling invites us to do far more than commit our life to paper. It guides us to ask the big questions that stories answer.

What is this life I'm living all about?

Who is the hero?

What did she overcome?

How did that change her?

Years ago, as a brand-new writer, I quit my job and spent a year traveling across the country in my Subaru Outback with a friend, as a way to "stir up" conflict in my very ordinary life. I knew I wanted to write something interesting, and I figured I needed to "make something interesting happen" in order to do that. As it turns out, my life was more interesting than I'd predicted it to be—even without the stunt of the road trip (although the road trip turned out to be a fun adventure I'm glad I took).

You don't need fantastical details to write an interesting story. You just need a unique perspective. And the lens of storytelling can give you exactly that.

SAME EVENTS, DIFFERENT INTERPRETATION

For years I would say to myself that the difference between life and the movies is that life doesn't resolve perfectly. But I was wrong. Life doesn't resolve until we *decide* how we'd like it to resolve. It doesn't resolve until we become the kind of person who can solve the hero's problem.

I'm not suggesting we can control all the outcomes of our lives. We can't. Sometimes in stories we get exactly what we *didn't* want. The money runs out, the cancer takes over, the friend or partner or loved one leaves, and there's nothing we can do but let it happen. The details of the story may be out of our control. The meaning we make of the story, however, is not.

Choosing to resolve your story is less about shifting your circumstances and more about deciding how you'd like to interpret them. Writing your story, unlike anything you've ever experienced before, will change the way you interpret the details of your life.

All those mornings I spent at the coffee shop writing about my divorce, I wasn't sure what I was doing exactly. I worried I was wasting my time. I knew I would "never publish" this kind of a story. Only now can I see what was happening under the surface. Only on the other side of writing can I see that the love I share with my now-husband and our two beautiful kids, even the work I do helping others shape their stories, was all born from my willingness to interpret some of the unwanted details of my life in a different way.

Back then, what it looked like I was doing was frenetically typing on my laptop in a coffee shop. But what I was really doing was evolving into the woman I am today.

A story framework is not everything. By itself it's not going to save your life. Neither is therapy or yoga or exercise or another inspiring book or podcast. But it can surely help shift your perspective. And sometimes even the slightest shift in perspective is all you need.

ONE THOUSAND STORIES

After college, my brother spent a decade in Hollywood working behind the scenes on movie and TV sets. One summer I went to visit him in LA while he was working on a popular reality TV show. He took me out to one of his favorite clubs, and a few cast members from a different reality show were playing pool there. I was barely twenty-one and starstruck.

On the drive home, I remember telling my brother how cool the night had been, how amazing it would be to live the life he was living, and how one day I wanted to be on TV too. I was young and naive, but I remember my notoriously laid-back brother getting stern with me and telling me that under no circumstances should I ever—EVER—agree to allow anyone to turn my life into a reality TV show.

"You probably won't get the opportunity," he said, "but if you do, promise me you'll turn it down." I didn't say anything. "There are a thousand stories you could tell about any one person," he said. "Don't give someone else the power to choose which one gets shared."

That conversation has never left me. Not because of reality TV. Because of what my brother said. *There are a thousand stories you could tell about any one person.* How you frame a life, how you choose to tell the stories of any one person, is what goes down in history. How you articulate a story is the way we all remember it.

Was your divorce the worst thing that ever happened to you, or the best? Was raising your children the hardest thing you've ever done, or the most joy-filled? The death of that loved one was tragic, absolutely, but wasn't it also the portal that opened you up to miracles and magic? You get to decide how the story is told and, therefore, how it is remembered—not just by you, but by anyone who reads it.

Whatever you do, don't leave the telling of your story to someone else. You can use a tool like storytelling to magnify the brilliance of your own existence. In order to do that, you'll need to know what your story is *really* about.

CHAPTER 3

What Is Your Story About? (The Controlling Idea)

My friend Jessie reached out to me because she wanted help writing her story. The only problem was, she wasn't sure exactly what her story was about. On the surface, the details were fairly cut-and-dried. One July day, on her way back from a romantic vacation for her anniversary, her husband and the father of her three children had a grand mal seizure. Within a few hours, he had been diagnosed with a large and aggressive brain tumor. Nine weeks later, he was gone.

Jessie and I sat together in my dining room nearly two years after Busbee, her husband, had passed away. As we talked about everything that had happened, we were trying to decide some things about her story:

- Was this a story about the brevity of life?
- Was it about the legacy we leave behind?

- Was it a complicated love story with a tragic but beautiful redemption?
- Was it about how people cope after someone they love is gone?

I told Jessie what I'll also tell you, which is that stories cannot be about *many* things. They have to be about *one* central thing, otherwise you (and your reader) will get lost. That central thing is called the Controlling Idea.

A Controlling Idea is, as it sounds, an idea that controls the shape of your story. The Controlling Idea will tell you what details to include in your story and which ones to leave out. It will dictate where the story begins and where it ends. It is the measuring stick against which you evaluate every element of the story. The Controlling Idea answers the question: What is this story about?

You'll know, for instance, that the problem or moral in your story is hitting the mark if it matches your Controlling Idea. You'll know if the resolution you chose adequately resolves the tension by setting it next to your Controlling Idea. You can measure your heroic transformation by looking back to your Controlling Idea. The Controlling Idea is your litmus test. And yet in order to use it that way, it has to be clearly defined.

The benefit of a Controlling Idea is extreme clarity. The challenge is defining such clarity for a nuanced story from your life. Getting this right can take some patience, but your diligence with this first element of the framework will pay off. When you write a great Controlling Idea, it becomes a lamppost, which will guide your writing and even, maybe, your life.

A Controlling Idea for a personal story looks like this:

This story is about . . . (THE HERO) who overcomes (THE ONE BIG PROBLEM) in order to experience (THE RESOLUTION).

That sentence may read like a foreign language to you right now, but I'll walk you through exactly how to understand each part of your story and how to write a Controlling Idea that will bring all the parts together.

Your story might seem like it is about many different things. It may appear to be about loss and heartbreak and abuse and childhood trauma and resilience and regret and joy and redemption. To write a Controlling Idea, you have to decide which of those things you want to prioritize. In storytelling, like in life, you cannot prioritize everything. You have to leave some things on the cutting room floor— even good things.

What is left after all that cutting? That's what your story is *really* about.

WHAT ONE STORY ARE YOU TELLING?

Before we can write your Controlling Idea together, we need to define what one story from your life you would like to write about. You have thousands of stories you could write. Infinite, really, since you are continually living new ones each day. You can eventually tell as many of those stories as you'd like. But for the purposes of learning this framework, we need to choose *one* story to start with.

- The story of your dad leaving
- The story of chasing down a dream
- The story of your divorce
- The story of welcoming home your children
- The story of getting the diagnosis
- The story of how you got your dream job
- The story of barely surviving that terrible thing
- The story of meeting your spouse and falling in love
- The story of your proudest moment or biggest success

Maybe you're like my friend Jessie, and you know *exactly* what story you're here to write. If you're not as sure, consider picking a story that has some charge for you.

When I say *charge*, I mean that the story has some electricity to it. When you talk about it, you might feel a little ungrounded or unsettled. Maybe even thinking about that time in your life makes you cry or makes your palms sweat or makes your heart speed up a little. If you have a physical reaction to a story, it's safe to say there's some charge to it. The bigger the charge to the story, the more opportunity there is for a resolution.

Part of the reason our stories live as a charge in our bodies is because the way we've told ourselves the story in the past—perhaps unconsciously—is out of alignment with what we know to be true in the present. Your body will always prompt you to update an old conclusion that isn't working for you anymore.

For instance, a story I felt prompted to write after years of feeling that charge in my body was the story of giving birth to my daughter, Nella. She was born in downtown Los Angeles in July 2020 at the height of a global pandemic. I was "supposed" to give birth at a birth center in Pasadena, where I lived, but Nella had other plans. My blood pressure skyrocketed at the last minute, so I had to give birth at the hospital. By the time she was born, I was so drugged and exhausted I hardly knew what was happening. And worse, Nella wasn't breathing when she arrived, so they took her to the NICU.

The story has a happy ending. My daughter is healthy and thriving and no worse for wear from her NICU stay (or being birthed in a hospital rather than in a birthing center). But for some reason, every time I tried to tell the story, I would feel an overwhelming heaviness come over me. I knew logically that everything was okay, but I felt like sobbing as if something terrible had happened.

It wasn't until I wrote the story that I figured out why.

As I wrote, I saw a meaning I had made about the story outside of my conscious awareness. I had been telling myself that the sudden turn of events around Nella's birth and the NICU stay was somehow a failure on my part; that if only I had been stronger, worked harder, or been more committed to my health during the pregnancy, the story could have turned out differently.

"I failed at my first task of being a mother," I wrote. As the words showed up on the page, I understood why I felt so much distress around this part of my life. I was telling myself the wrong story.

As it relates to the birth of my daughter, the charge was my body's way of nudging me to rewrite the story. It was my body's way of saying *that* belief is not going to take you where you want to go. Let's unearth this narrative so we can update the moral.

I did update it. The story I tell myself now is that it was my body's innate intelligence and my willingness to listen that saved our lives that day. If my blood pressure hadn't skyrocketed at that exact moment, and if I hadn't wisely allowed the transfer to the hospital, Nella and I both might have died. My daughter spoke, and I listened, and our combined wisdom guided us both in the right direction.

My first big success as a mother.

While it's true that a highly charged event will lead to an interesting story and a satisfying resolution, only you can decide how much charge is too much charge for you to tackle. You always have your hand on the dial of how far you'd like to go. You can start with something small, dip your toe in the water, play with a story, take a break when you need to, and bite off chunks as you go. You may decide that writing a story with a lot of charge feels too overwhelming for you. That's fine. Choose something with less charge.

You're also welcome to dive into the deep end of your life if that sounds appealing—or healing—to you.

Whatever you do, choose an event that is specific and finite. Rather than "the story of losing my father," maybe you tell the story of the burial service. Instead of "the story of my career as a teacher" maybe you focus on the day you received recognition for being Teacher of the Year. Remember, the goal is to write a story three to five pages long. Eventually, you can write more than one story and turn it into a collection of essays or a memoir if you want. But for the sake of this process, starting with a specific event will feel much more manageable.

Choosing a single and specific story to work with as you learn the framework will help you go beyond intellectually understanding stories and actually practice putting one together. Once you understand this framework and how it operates, you'll be equipped to use it over and over again to write the many stories you have to share.

What *one* story do you want to write first?

WHAT IS YOUR STORY ABOUT?

You might think you already know what your story is about ("it's about my divorce" or "it's about losing everything and rebuilding"), but what is your story *really* about? Who is the story about? What difficulties did that person have to overcome inside the story? How did that person transform as a result of those challenges? Answering these three questions is foundational to writing your Controlling Idea and therefore determining the arc of your story.

1. **Who** is the story about?
2. **What** did that person overcome?
3. **How** did that person change?

When Jessie sat with me in my dining room that day, this is exactly the process I walked through with her. We started by defining *who* the story was about.

It was tempting for Jessie to think her story might be about her late husband. So much of what took place had to do with him and his tumor. Besides, he was a well-known figure in the music industry, and much of Jessie's life had revolved around his charisma and career. In some ways he seemed like the obvious central character to the story. But this story was not about him. It was about Jessie.

I'll say the same to you. Assuming you're using this framework the way it was intended—to write a story from your life—the story is about *you*. You are the main character of the story, or the hero.

I unpack this in more depth in Chapter 5, so I won't spend too much time on it here. But if you're anything like Jessie, or most of the writers who come to our workshops, you might feel a smidge uncomfortable calling yourself the hero.

Culturally, we use the word *hero* to describe a person who gives up his or her own life or freedom to protect or serve someone else. War veterans are heroes. Firefighters are heroes. First responders are heroes. Single moms are heroes.

When we're talking about heroes in stories, though, the word means something a little bit different. Heroes in stories are notoriously unheroic for most of the story. They are typically mixed-up and directionless, self-doubting and confused. They often make the same wrong choices over and over again. Their big heroic moment comes at the very end of the story, in the last scene, right before the whole thing ends.

To be the hero of a story, you don't need to risk your own life to save someone else's. To be the hero of a story, you just need to be a person who has been mixed-up and confused, who has made some wrong choices or taken some wrong turns, who questions yourself and lacks confidence at times, and who genuinely has the desire to grow and change.

To be the hero of a story, you just need to be a person who has been mixed-up and confused, who has made some wrong choices and who genuinely has the desire to grow and change.

To put yourself at the center of your story does not mean putting yourself at the epicenter of human existence. It simply means putting yourself at the center of your business success or your divorce or your experience losing someone you loved. There will be other characters, yes. But you *are* at the center. Who else could be? You are the character the reader is following. You are the one who struggles. You are the one who moves the plot forward. You are the one who transforms.

You are the hero.

In order to write your Controlling Idea, we need to know more than just that you *are* the hero of the story. We need to know a little bit about what you were like at the beginning of the story. The arc of the story is built around the hero's transformation, so we need to define something: Who were you when all of this started?

- A happy, carefree man who didn't know loss?
- A searching young woman who didn't see how confused she was?
- An insecure man who was unaware of his impact on others?
- A naive young woman who trusted others too much?
- A driven, ambitious person who lacked faith in something bigger than himself?
- A rigid, perfectionistic human who couldn't handle failure?

Defining who you were in the beginning of the story is going to help you determine the transformation of the hero, which is a key element of your Controlling Idea.

WHAT IS THE OBSTACLE?

Once you've nailed down the *who*, you are ready to move on to the *what*. What did your hero have to overcome inside the story? On the surface, your answer may be obvious. It might be something like divorce, bankruptcy, a traumatic upbringing, anxiety, or your own insecurity. Or perhaps, like Jessie, you had to overcome the loss of a loved one. Whatever your specific obstacle was, consider how you can make it as *tangible* as possible.

If the obstacle you had to overcome was insecurity, for instance, how did that insecurity show up in the world? Did you sabotage a good relationship? Did you lose a job you loved because you were always competing instead of collaborating? Did you push away someone who was trying to help you?

Remember the story I shared earlier in this chapter about giving birth to my daughter? We could, in one way, define the obstacle of that story as my own internal feeling of failure. I transformed inside the story from feeling like I had failed as a mom to seeing myself as a remarkable success. At the same time, the story doesn't work without the physical, tangible obstacle of birth itself. Feeling like a failure is an *idea*, but an unexpected turn of events in childbirth is a *story*. *That's* the obstacle.

Take a minute to think about the physical, tangible obstacle in *your* story. If you're not sure if the obstacle is tangible enough, ask yourself what the obstacle would look like on a movie screen. How would you know the hero of the story was struggling?

At one of our Write Your Story workshops, we had a participant named Grant, who came to write a story about overcoming his anxiety. Anxiety is certainly a big obstacle. But I encouraged Grant to think about how to make this obstacle even more physical. As we unpacked his story, Grant mentioned that he had been suffering from panic attacks. He could pinpoint the exact moments when these panic attacks happened and describe them in vivid detail.

I encouraged Grant to use the panic attacks—rather than his anxiety—as the obstacle because it would make it easier for him to organize his story and make sense of it. Which can you better picture on a movie screen: anxiety or panic attacks?

Cheryl Strayed's memoir *Wild* follows the hero of the story as she hikes the Pacific Crest Trail after losing her mom to cancer. In an attempt to cope with her overwhelming grief, she decides to take on one of the longest hikes in the world—spanning from the southern tip of California to the northernmost point of Washington—despite having little to no hiking experience. It's the *physical* obstacle of the trail that makes her story so compelling. And, as a side note, it is also what made it work so well as a movie.

You can *see* the long hike on a screen in a way you can't see the grief of a woman who had just lost her mom.

A story about a woman drowning in grief is interesting, but not as interesting as a story about a woman drowning in grief who takes on a physical challenge like the PCT. Can you see how the physicality of the hike helps us, the readers, to connect with the internal struggles the hero faces? What's your story's equivalent to the Pacific Crest Trail?

I'm not suggesting you alter the true-to-life details of your story to make it more compelling for Hollywood (although that could be a fun exercise). What I'm suggesting is that you think past the internal struggles of the hero to consider how her obstacle could be incarnated in the physical world.

Let's think back to your story. What did you overcome? How can you take your internal struggle and make it as visible as possible?

Here are some ideas inspired by past workshop participants:

- Five bucks in the checking account
- Divorce papers sitting on your counter
- A blank test sheet (your last chance to pass) sitting in front of you
- A knife at your throat
- An eight-month trip down a river
- A year overseas (when you've never left home)
- The brain scans from the doctor
- A positive pregnancy test

Notice the energy you feel as you read these obstacles. It's much easier to connect. The more tangible you can be in your Controlling Idea, the easier it will be to write your story. The words are going to come more easily, the process will feel more fluid, and you'll be less likely to lose track of what the story is truly about.

To write your story is to do more than just take an event from your life and put it down on paper. It's considering your experience more deeply. It's acknowledging to yourself that there is both a feeling on the inside and an obstacle that manifests itself out in the world. It's paying attention to the connections and patterns you see there.

It's putting on the glasses and seeing yourself in the mirror clearly, perhaps for the first time.

HOW DOES THE STORY RESOLVE?

We're not quite to a solid Controlling Idea yet, but the story is beginning to take shape. You're starting to see your arc coming through. To complete your Controlling Idea, the last question we need to answer is this: How does the story resolve?

Personal stories resolve when the hero changes. Period.

If at the beginning of the story the hero is "broken," by the end of the story we need to see her healed. Or, at the very least, we need to see her revise her definition of "broken." If a man is insecure at the beginning of the story, we want him to become confident by the end. That resolution completes the arc of the story.

You could make an argument that stories resolve once the hero gets what they had wanted at the beginning of the story. That *is* a common way for stories to resolve. The guy gets the girl. The officer subdues the terrorist and saves the hostages. The struggling artist finally catches her big break.

But when it comes to personal stories, there's a reason to prioritize heroic transformation over the simple resolution of the problem. Transformation is what ushers in any physical resolution. The transformation of the hero is exactly how the hero gets the girl or catches the big break. One is not possible without the other.

When *we* shift, our circumstances shift.

But what about when you're stuck without an obvious resolution?

Personal stories are unique in that you can't just write any old ending to the story. It has to be true to how things actually happened.

Many times, writers show up at a Write Your Story workshop without a clear resolution to their story. Personal stories are unique in that you can't just write any old ending to the story. It has to be true to how things actually happened. Wouldn't it be nice if you could just write a happy "guy gets girl" kind of ending to your story and your life would follow suit?

And yet, as nice as it sounds to write your own conclusion, consider for a moment that the happy ending you would write for your story might not be as magical as the one that gets written when you focus on heroic transformation. The ending isn't always "cancer gets cured" or "wife comes back." Sometimes we have to find a way to look beyond the physical characteristics of the story to uncover what our life is trying to show us.

What might your life be trying to show you?

THE CONTROLLING IDEA

Jessie is still working on her Controlling Idea. She's still making important decisions about what her story is *exactly* about. She's still waiting for more clarity on the resolution. It's ok to take your time writing your Controlling Idea. It's okay, normal even, to play with it for a while, see what fits, take it for a test run, and then come back to edit it again later. Your Controlling Idea will guide your entire writing process, so it makes sense for you to want to get it just right.

To get started writing your own Controlling Idea, start by answering these three questions separately:

- Who is this story about? (THE HERO)
- What does that person overcome? (THE ONE BIG PROBLEM)
- How does that person change? (THE RESOLUTION)

After you've done that, experiment with dropping your three answers into this formula:

This story is about . . . (THE HERO) who overcomes (THE ONE BIG PROBLEM) in order to experience (THE RESOLUTION).

Here are some examples from past workshop participants:

- **This story is about** a broke single mom (THE HERO) who goes from having five bucks in her pocket (THE ONE BIG PROBLEM) to building a multi-six-figure business (THE RESOLUTION).
- **This story is about** a husband and father of three children (THE HERO) who is given two years to live (THE ONE BIG PROBLEM) and reorients his priorities to fill the final years of his life with presence and awe (THE RESOLUTION).
- **This story is about** a young woman who suffered unimaginable abuse (THE HERO) and, after watching her daughter suffer at the hands of the same person (THE PROBLEM), realizes that not everyone deserves her loyalty or trust (THE RESOLUTION).
- **This story is about** a vibrant young woman (THE HERO) who loses not one but two husbands in tragic accidents (THE PROBLEM) and discovers what pain and loss and grief have to teach about the beauty of life (THE RESOLUTION).
- **This is a story about** a washed-up athlete (THE HERO) who fights for months to pass the LSAT (THE ONE BIG PROBLEM) to achieve his dream of becoming a lawyer (THE RESOLUTION).

A well-written Controlling Idea will guide your writing process. You can come back to this important phrase again and again and ask yourself *Does this certain piece of information belong in the story, or should I delete it?* When you find an element that doesn't fit, you have one of two choices: you can leave it out, or you can go back to your Controlling Idea and edit.

You likely won't get your Controlling Idea right on the first swing. But that isn't the goal. The goal is to have something to guide your way as you move through the rest of the framework. If something in the story doesn't seem to be working, the Controlling Idea is almost always the culprit. I like to joke that you write your entire story as a way to get your Controlling Idea right. Then you go back and write your story again.

Is your story about love or loss? Is it about the death of your mom, or is it about the many things we lose in this lifetime? Is it about getting swindled, or is it about letting go of that childlike naïveté? Or perhaps it is about grappling with a big question like Is the world a safe place?

Every detail in the story, every theme, every aspect of the story, has to align with the Controlling Idea; otherwise, clarity is lost. The Controlling Idea keeps you on track.

THE COST OF CLARITY

We aren't very good at seeing ourselves clearly. It's unfortunate but true. This is why we have to hire therapists (thank

God for therapists) and pay them hundreds or thousands of dollars to help us see. Please just help us see! Sometimes even when they spell it out, we still don't want to open our eyes. Clarity is not always easy.

When it comes to personal stories, getting clarity costs us something. It costs us options! The story could have "resolved" in a dozen different ways. We could have given it ten other meanings. But instead, we're giving it this one.

And yet notice how peaceful it feels to get clear on something. My husband and I had been having the same tense discussion over and over again for months because we were misunderstanding each other. Just the other day we had a breakthrough. I wasn't really listening to him! Once I got clarity, a huge weight was lifted. We still didn't agree, but I understood him, and having that clarity changed everything.

Moviegoers pay billions of dollars each year to see what is, essentially, the same couple of movies over and over again. I'm more predictable than all of those moviegoers combined. When I've had a long day, I watch *Friends* or *Gilmore Girls* for the seven hundredth time because I know exactly what to expect.

Clarity can be incredibly healing.

Can you allow the Controlling Idea of your story to give you some of the clarity you are craving? Like a good therapist, urging you to see, can you let your story show you something you haven't yet been able to see?

Stories thrive on clarity. It's why we love them so much—and it's why writing your story is healing. Because stories bring clarity to the chaos of our minds.

Stories bring clarity to the chaos of our minds.

"Life isn't that cut-and-dried!" people tell me. And I get it. I've said this to myself a time or two while writing. I'm not suggesting you short-circuit the intricacies of your life to make an interesting piece of art. I'm suggesting you receive fully the clarity that is trying to come to you. Don't make things more complicated than they need to be.

What story are you writing, and what is that story about? It can't be about ten things. It has to be about one thing. Can you allow yourself to get crystal clear on what you're trying to say? Can you write the story ten different ways and then ask yourself which one you like best?

Whatever you write doesn't have to be set in stone. You can practice with something and edit as you go. But allow the act of writing your story to give you the gift of clarity. Once you are able to do that, you're ready to begin.

CHAPTER 4

How to Find the Hook
(The Opening Line)

Many people worry that their story isn't interesting enough to grip a reader's attention. Even if fascinating things have happened to them, they worry that the details must only be interesting to them. Why would anyone else care? Who would ever read this? Before you write off your story as boring or uninspiring, consider that you might be holding back the most fascinating parts about yourself.

What if the most interesting part about you and your story is something you would never think to share?

A young man whom I'll call James came to one of our Write Your Story workshops wanting to write about a three-month-long solo camping trip he took. For the entire first day of the workshop, he talked about the obstacles he'd faced out in the wilderness and what those obstacles had taught him. You could tell he had a deep reverence for nature, which was interesting in its own way.

But it wasn't until the second day that someone thought to ask James what made him go on the camping trip in the first place. That's when we learned it was because his sister had been killed in a drunk driving accident.

What if the most interesting part about you and your story is something you would never think to share?

"Going into the woods is what kept me from going to jail," he joked.

What he meant was that the three months in nature is what helped him find peace and forgiveness so that he would avoiding *murdering* his sister's killer. Now, James didn't actually have plans to murder anyone. But he knew he needed some way to process the rage he felt for what had happened to someone he loved. He was furious about what had been taken from his family forever. Hence his three-month sojourn into the woods.

Talk about burying the lead. Think of how this hidden piece of information could unlock James's story, if he had thought to tell it.

What is the piece of information you're holding back that could unlock yours?

FINDING A HOOK

Finding the "hook" of a story is about deciding what makes the story interesting. Establishing the foundation of *interest* enables you to know where the story should begin, write a strong opening line, and carry the reader's attention from the first word of the story to the final resolution. No turning away. No distractions.

You might think to yourself, *Well, that's nice, but I'm not writing a movie script here. This is a story from my life.* Fair point. But consider that guiding a reader's attention inside of a narrative is about way more than just keeping that reader entertained. It's about *connection*. It's about recognizing that this story you are writing and living is not only about you. It's about others who are paying attention.

Have you ever had the experience where you hear a great story and are captivated from the very beginning? It can feel like you're pulled into a journey outside of yourself, almost like an out-of-body experience. That's because, in a way, you *are* pulled into a journey beyond yourself. This out-of-body experience is called Narrative Transportation.

Narrative Transportation is the idea that stories change us. Not metaphorically but literally. When we hear a great story, we grow and change right along with the hero of the story. If the hero goes from self-doubting to confident, so do we. If the hero goes from arrogant to humble, so do we. If the hero goes from scared to brave, *so do we.* Stories are not just stories. They are also vehicles for growth and evolution.

When you learn how to not just write a story but also to *share* a story with readers, the gift you get in return is connection. Your struggle is their struggle. Your transformation is their transformation. You are not alone.

When you learn how to share a story with readers, the gift you get in return is connection. Your struggle is their struggle. Your transformation is their transformation. You are not alone.

If you still worry that your story isn't gripping enough to interest anyone, here is something to consider: it's possible you're hiding the most interesting part of your story like James did, and it's also possible that you're not allowing the most fascinating details of your story to unfold in the first place.

Sometimes we get into writing a story from our lives and realize we have been tiptoeing around the very things that give stories a hook in the first place: Tension. Conflict. Upheaval. Falling-apart.

If you're afraid to ask a question you don't have the answer to, if you're avoiding stepping out onto a path that doesn't have a clear foreseeable end, if you're afraid to do something completely out of the ordinary for you because you don't know how things will turn out, you might be avoiding the story instead of really living it. A story where the hero refuses to enter the action will always lack the intrigue we crave.

There are times in life to accept a boring story. I'm not suggesting we drum up drama for the sake of drama. What I *am* suggesting is that your life might be trying to give you a hook, and you might be resisting it.

Seeing where in your life you are hiding or avoiding the hook is one of the many ways writing your story will heal your life, if you let it. Writing about your life will show you where the story is stuck. It will shine a light on what you're avoiding: having the hard conversation, speaking the truth, getting up on the stage, saying yes, saying no, setting the boundary, releasing the tightly held grip.

These would all be fascinating hooks. Are you brave enough to let the story unfold the way it is trying to unfold?

When people tell me they're worried that their story isn't all that interesting to other people, what I think they're really telling me is that they worry their story isn't interesting to *them*. When I worry that my own life isn't captivating, it's almost always because I've lost track of the arc of the story. I've let the seemingly unrelated details rise above the most important ones. I've tiptoed around the questions and the tension.

A hook cuts right through the noise. A hook asks a question that the reader *needs* to answer. A hook sets your hero on a clear path.

THE CLEAR PATH

Your opening line does more than give the reader an entry point to your story—it also sets a path for the hero to follow. That first line carries the weight of not only engaging the reader's attention but also suggesting where the story is about to go.

Imagine that I threw a baseball across the room to you. Assuming you have seen a ball thrown a handful of times in your life, you will be able to make a rough estimate of where the ball is going to land. The same is true with stories. If I have a basic understanding of how stories work, I can read an opening line (or a couple of lines) and make a pretty good guess about where the story will "land."

Sometimes the assumptions a reader makes at the beginning of a story are wrong, just like if you tried to catch the ball I threw but misjudged its trajectory for any number of reasons. The point is not that the reader guesses every detail (or "catches" the ball). The point is that that opening line gives the reader a clear path to follow—the arc.

Let me give you a sense of what I mean by this with a simple exercise. Take a look at your bookshelf and select one, two, or three books that are story-driven, like a memoir or a novel. As long as you're not looking at a textbook or a self-help book, the opening line will read something like these examples taken from my bookshelf:

I'm seven years old, talking to myself, because I'm scared, and because I'm the only person who listens to me. Under my breath I whisper: Just quit, Andre, just give up. Put down your racket and walk off this court, right now. Go into the house and get something good to eat. Play with Rita, Philly, or Tami. Sit with mom while she knits or does her jigsaw puzzle. Doesn't that sound nice? Wouldn't that feel like heaven, Andre? To just quit? To never play tennis again? (First paragraph of Chapter 1 from *Open* by Andre Agassi)[1]

It's strange how we always give big news to loved ones in a coma, as if a coma is just a thing that happens from a lack of something to be excited about in your life. Mom is in the ICU at the hospital. The doctor told us she has forty-eight hours to live. Grandma, Grandpa, and Dad are out in the waiting room calling relatives and eating vending machine snacks. Grandma says Nutter Butters soothe her anxiety. (First two paragraphs of the Prologue from *I'm Glad My Mom Died* by Jeannette McCurdy)[2]

When I broached the subject with my father, when I worked up the nerve to tell him about my Crazy Idea, I made sure it was early in the evening. That was always the best time with Dad. He was relaxed then, well fed, stretched out in his vinyl recliner in the TV nook. I can still tilt back my head and close my eyes and hear the sound of the audience laughing, the tinny theme songs of his favorites shows, *Wagon Train* and *Rawhide*. (First paragraph of "1962" from *Shoe Dog* by Phil Knight)[3]

On July 13, 2013, the night of my brother's wedding, I left my four-year-old daughter alone in a hotel room because I was blackout drunk. It shouldn't have been a surprise, but it was—to me, to my family, to my friends who found out later. I had a twenty-year history with alcohol and sometimes it looked problematic, but mostly—except for the last couple of years, and even then only if you got *really* close—things looked normal enough. (First few sentences of the Introduction from *We Are the Luckiest* by Laura McKowen)[4]

You'll notice from these examples and the ones you pull from your own bookshelf how many assumptions you can make from the first few lines of an author's story. That first entry point not only cuts through the confusion but also grabs a reader's attention. It "lobs" a metaphorical ball, and now, as the reader, you are fixated on where that ball is going to go. When you set the trajectory for your reader, what you're really saying to them is "I know where I'm going with this." A passenger doesn't want to ride in a car with someone who doesn't know where they're driving, and a reader doesn't want to read a story where the narrator doesn't know where the story is going to land. While you don't want the narrator to give away all the secrets in that first line, you do want to feel as if there is a destination in mind.

As a quick review, your opening line needs to:

- Open the story
- Grip a reader's attention
- Reveal the most interesting part about your story (what your story is *really* about)
- Set the arc (giving a hint to the destination)

If I were writing an opening line for James's story, I'd write something like this:

Nine days after losing my sister, I entered those woods. I would be a different man when I came out.

In two short sentences an author can grip a reader's attention, set up the arc of the story, show the reader that the narrator knows where he is going, and clearly define what the story is about.

It's a tall order for the first line (or few lines) of your story—one you may not know how to fill quite yet. But for now, it's a question worth considering: Where do you want this story to go?

THE QUESTIONS THAT HOOK US

There are a handful of "tricks" you can use to quickly learn how to write a strong opening line. I could list them here. And yet almost all of the opening line tactics (which you could also Google search, by the way) can be boiled down to this: you hook your reader by getting them to ask a question.

Questions are *very* motivating to the human brain. Consider the last time you saw someone you knew at the grocery store but forgot their name. For hours (or until you remember) your brain is on repeat: *What is their name? What is their name?*

How about when you're scrolling on your phone late at night and see a headline like, "The one thing all parents do to screw up their kids . . ." You were *supposed* to be going to bed. Instead, for the next fifteen minutes, your brain is hijacked. It wants to get the answer to the question. What is the *one* thing? And are you doing it?

The term "open loop" comes from psychologist Bluma Zeigarnik, who was the first to discover that our brains are more likely to focus on a task that is unfinished than one that is finished.[5] Translated to storytelling, this means your brain is wired to pay attention to an "open" story and to turn your focus *away* when a story is finished or resolved.

Writing an opening line that hooks your reader and pulls them into the story is about asking a question in the first line that you don't fully answer until the last word. Sometimes you do this by literally opening the story with an interesting question: *How long does it take to repair a broken spirit? I've spent my whole life trying to figure it out.*

And yet you don't have to literally ask a question to "open" a story in your reader's mind. Take James's example from earlier. If James tells the reader that he entered the woods nine days after his sister died and then left three months later a changed man—what question is the reader asking herself?

She's asking: *How* did that happen? The author will then spend the rest of the story focused on answering that one question.

What question is your story asking?

I want to emphasize that opening a story loop doesn't just keep a reader engaged in the story. It also keeps *you* engaged. When you clearly define the question your story is asking, you are able to bring focused energy to closing the loop.

As you think about the hook of your story, why not use the questions you're already asking yourself?

- How do I overcome this heartbreak and move on?
- What do I believe about God / heaven / hell / life after death?
- What if I lose everything?
- Does my life have a purpose?
- Will I ever heal my anxiety?
- How would I survive a financial collapse?
- Do kids suffer when their parents divorce?
- Why are some people successful and others aren't?
- Will she leave or will she stay?
- Should I quit my job?

What are the questions that keep you up at night? What open loops get you out of bed in the morning? What problem drives you crazy that you can't seem to solve? Ask yourself what gets your brain "hooked" and maybe you'll find the hook to your story.

WHERE DOES YOUR STORY BEGIN?

Usually, the "beginning" of the story isn't the actual beginning. Let's say you're writing the story of your business collapse and what it taught you. Which part seems most like the beginning?

1. Your childhood: being bullied at school; having a driven dad who pushed you
2. The moment you got the business idea: the flash of insight; feeling pulled or called
3. Getting the bankruptcy letter in the mail: the crushing shame and despair you felt

There's no one right answer here, but as a general rule you want to enter your story at the point of greatest possible tension. In this case, number 3 has that tension.

Usually, your childhood isn't the place to enter the story, as interesting as the details may be. The details of your childhood may be a helpful way to provide some backstory to the hero (see chapter 5), but childhood is not the beginning of the story.

The beginning of the story is where we find the hero in over her head, due either to her own choices or the choices of someone else. The story begins when the hero is pushed into a new reality, an unfamiliar world, an experience she does not know how to navigate.

The question that drives your story could be as simple as:

- How will the hero get through this?
- What will happen next?

The point of the most possible tension is not just a reader's entry point into the story; it's also the author's. It's often when a writer nails down the entry point to their story that it suddenly clicks for them what the story is actually about. No longer are you drowning in a thousand details. You're singularly focused on a clear question: *How will this all resolve?* Or perhaps, *What will the hero do next?*

I find it fascinating how even the most inexperienced writers are, without fail, quite good at coming up with an opening line when they sit down to think about it. We do this intuitively, I've found. We say things like, "Guess who I bumped into at the grocery store last night?" We understand that the questions are sometimes more interesting than the answers, that gripping someone into a story is as important as telling the story itself.

ASKING BETTER QUESTIONS

Not all questions are created equal. If the question that has you "hooked" in your life doesn't take you on a very interesting journey, consider that it might be time to try asking a better question. For example, I find that "why" questions are often a dead-end street:

1. Why did my mom die?
2. Why did I miscarry?
3. Why couldn't he love me?
4. Why do I have anxiety?
5. Why can't the sky be pink?

Sometimes we need to ask the why questions. It's part of our process as human beings. We want to understand. And yet the answers to the why question can be dissatisfying. Why did my mom die? *Because she did.* Why couldn't he love me? *Because he couldn't.* Why can't the sky be pink? *Because that's not the way it is.* This is not a hard and fast rule but a pattern I've noticed as I've worked with hundreds of writers to help them take an event from their life and turn it into a story.

Why questions are not nearly the fire starters for stories that *how* or *who* or *what* questions are.

1. **How** would I have to look at this story differently to see what it's trying to show me?
2. **Who** would I have to become, as the hero, for this loop to close?

3. **What** am I missing about this set of circumstances that would allow me to experience it differently?

The better the questions we ask, the better the stories we are going to tell. If you're asking a question like "Why am I in so much pain all the time?" your brain will work tirelessly to answer that question. It might find an answer for you—like maybe something you're doing isn't good for you. That can be helpful. But what if you asked other questions: "How can I find peace?" or "What creates freedom for people?"

The better the questions we ask, the better the stories we are going to tell.

Wouldn't the answer to the *what* and *how* questions provide an even more useful conclusion?

When I was writing the story of my divorce, I started by asking the question "Why is this happening to me?" and others like it. That's fine. That's where I needed to begin. Over time, however, I upgraded my questions. I started asking, "What does this make possible?" And, "How can I see myself as an empowered hero of the story?" When I did that, my life began to change.

There was a certain satisfaction I thought I might gain from understanding why, but there came a point when I didn't need to know why anymore. Instead, I wanted to know, *What's next for me? How can I rise above this? What does my future look like, and how can I participate in bringing it to pass?*

You may not feel ready to upgrade your questions, but if you do, the result can be profound. Questions are motivating. Our brains don't give up on questions until they're answered. How could you use a vehicle like better questions to take your brain where you'd prefer it to go?

OTHER IDEAS FOR AN OPENING LINE

There are, of course, other ways to open a story loop besides asking a question. One way is to make a bold statement that requires further explanation. A Write Your Story workshop participant wrote this as her opening line: "I came within seven days of marrying a psychopath." You couldn't possibly read this opening line and then walk away from the story, uninterested. Instead, you're wondering:

- *You did?*
- How did that happen?
- Were there any red flags, or were you blindsided?
- How did you get out?
- Do you feel safe now?
- How did you recover?

These questions, which are never even explicitly stated in the text, do all the work of pulling the reader through the rest of her narrative.

Your opening line doesn't have to be as dramatic as nearly marrying a psychopath. You could open with a statement of belief, for example. You might say something that would surprise the reader, or confuse them. What about this for an opening line?

I now believe people are mostly good.

The "now" in the above statement assumes a "before" that the author doesn't directly mention. Again, this opening line doesn't literally ask a question, but it does beg a few:

1. What did you believe before?
2. What made you believe that people *weren't* mostly good?
3. What happened to you that changed your belief?

If making a bold statement doesn't seem to fit your story, you could also hook your reader by dropping them directly into the middle of the conflict. What if the opening line of your story described you sitting on the pavement, head in your hands, fingers wet with tears, no idea where you were going to go next? What if the opening line described you reaching into your pocket to grasp a five-dollar bill—the only money you had left to your name?

Ask yourself how you could take the reader directly into the middle of the pain or the challenge of your story right there in that opening line.

One Write Your Story participant dropped us into the middle of his story where he was staring at a VHS tape on his shelf, deciding if he wanted to watch it. I still remember that opening line to this day. I *had* to know.

What is on the VHS tape?

Another participant took a comic approach to an opening line and described walking into a public restroom to find a man with no pants. The hidden questions driving this story are

- Who is this man?
- Where are his pants?
- What is going to happen next?

No matter what strategy you use to get your reader's attention, the underlying objective is always the same: open a loop in the reader's brain to pull them into the story. The opening line gets the reader to ask the question "What's going to happen next?" And it ensures they won't give up until they find the answer.

CHAPTER 5

Setting the Anchor (The Hero Who Wants Something)

Svetka reached out to me because she wanted to write her story and needed some help. When I asked her what the story was about, she told me it was about her mother and her grandmother—two people who had inspired her to become the woman she was today. I knew that, if it was really *Svetka's* story, it couldn't be *about* her mother and her grandmother, so I kept asking questions to see if I could get to the Controlling Idea.

It all started when she stood at her mother's deathbed, Svetka told me (a great hook). Before that moment, she hadn't shown much interest in her mother's life, her history, her upbringing, her faith, her way of seeing the world. And yet, as she watched her mother's body slowly waste away, it occurred to her that this might be the last chance she would get to learn about the woman who had raised her.

While she sat with her mom in those final days, Svetka began asking questions. And while she *did* gain small bits of insight—why her mom had chosen to move from the former Soviet Union to the United States, for example, and the reasons that faith had been such an important part of her journey—her mother passed before Svetka could get all the answers she was looking for. In her mother's absence, Svetka's thirst for knowledge became unquenchable. She *had* to know more about who she was and where she came from. So she began digging.

Svetka traveled to two different US states and back to Russia to interview relatives and a friend of her grandmother's, a fellow Gulag survivor, who could answer her many questions about her mother and, eventually, her maternal grandmother. She uncovered an entire history she'd never known existed, including her grandmother's forgotten letters, previously recorded interviews, and archived concentration camp registration papers from 1940s' Germany.

She collected pages and pages of information, which she shared with me as we spoke. The details of her story were truly compelling. At the same time, I saw something that made me pause. There were multiple storylines taking place—namely, her mom's storyline and her grandmother's storyline—which muddled Svetka's writing.

Who was this story *truly* about?

Stories need a central character (or sometimes a group of characters, like a sports team); otherwise, the reader doesn't know who to follow. When this character doesn't exist, it's impossible to find the arc, and the story structure breaks down. We lose interest, both as the writer and the reader when we can't find the thread that holds the whole thing together.

When a story has an anchor character, it focuses our attention. We tune in to the one person who is going to change. We're able to enter the story through Narrative Transportation and participate in the hero's transformation. We settle into the story's one central perspective and cohesive narration The story might not offer us the Truth about everything that has ever existed in the world, but that's not what we're looking for. We read stories to get *one* character's point of view.

There are stories that follow multiple heroic characters and have multiple character arcs. But those stories are *fiction* because they require an omniscient narrator. They require a storyteller who can get inside the psyche of every character in the story and understand what motivates them. If you can read people's minds, you can have multiple heroes in your story. If not, you'll need to choose a singular heroic character and—I'm not sorry to say—that hero is you.

I told Svetka that if it were true she wanted to write *her* story, then this story was going to need to be about— surprise, surprise—*her*. What I meant is that she'd be centered in the middle of this story. Her mother and grandmother would still play important roles, but the story would be about a young woman (Svetka), who wanted to understand who she was and where she came from, and who went on a journey to learn something important.

As for the "important" thing Svetka learned, she'd have to tease that out as she wrote the story.

Svetka shared her reservations. "My grandmother was put in prison for her faith and served several years in a Siberian gulag as well a Nazi labor camp. How can I be the hero? It feels disrespectful to call myself a hero."

I assured her there was no pressure and that, if she didn't feel comfortable making herself the hero of the story, she could find another way to write it. (She could write it as historical fiction, for example, but then it wouldn't be *her* story; it would be her grandmother's story.) But before we hung up the phone, I reminded her that being the hero of the story didn't mean she was the strongest character in the story—or even the most important. It simply meant she was the one who the reader was tracking.

She was the one who wanted something (to know where she came from). She was the one who would face obstacles (a dying mother, a history fading away). She was the one who would transform (from fearful to courageous, perhaps).

"How did this journey change you?" I asked. She nodded at my question but wasn't sure how to answer it. A few minutes later we said goodbye, and I hung up the phone.

The next time we talked, Svetka told me she had shared parts of her early writing with a friend. Her friend commented, "This is good, Svetka, but I want to know more about what you think and feel about all of this. You're telling me a lot of information about your mother and grandmother, but I want to see your grandmother through your eyes, to connect with you as the character."

"You were right," Svetka said. "I keep trying to pretend like I'm not the center of this story, but it's impossible. Of course I'm the center. I'm the one putting all the pieces together. I'm the one who is making the meaning. Now I understand what you meant when you said I need to be the hero." Since then, Svetka has not only been able to uncover what her story is about, she's also turning it into a book titled *The Women Who Came before Me*.

You can't tell your story until you're willing to make yourself the hero.

You can't tell your story until you're willing to make yourself the hero. It doesn't mean there aren't other wise and beautiful characters in your story (you have guides, for example, which I'll address in Chapter 7). It doesn't mean you're the most important person in the world. It simply means that this story follows your perspective, your shift. You are the one and only person who can make meaning of it all.

THE HERO OR THE SIDEKICK?

Cindy came to one of our Write Your Story workshops after having recently walked with her best friend through two years of cancer treatments, only to watch her wither away and eventually die. Cindy was beside herself and wanted to write the story as a way to find some healing.

The only problem was, Cindy was adamant she wasn't the hero of this story. I tried all of my usual explanations, but she wouldn't budge. She insisted that her friend Peggy was the heroic one.

I gave Cindy space during the first day because it seemed like she needed it. On the second day, when she grew frustrated that her story wasn't working, I asked if she'd be willing to at least *try* putting herself in the position of the hero to see what might happen. We didn't have to keep it that way. We could just play with the details for now. What would this story be about if it *was* about Cindy?

She wasn't sure.

"What did you want at the beginning of this story that you couldn't have?" I asked Cindy, and she immediately softened. Tears streamed down her face. She looked down at her page. When she looked up a minute later, she squeaked out an answer.

"I wanted to save my friend."

I turned to the group and asked, "How many of you want to read a story about a woman who wished she could save someone she loves . . . but couldn't?" The room was dead silent but every hand went up. I saw several people wiping away tears.

I told Cindy that if she wanted to write Peggy's story, that was fine. She could use the same framework I was teaching and try to map out a story about a woman who fought cancer and went bravely, all the way to the grave. That's a remarkable story. But *her* story was also beautiful, I told her. And *her* story was where she would uncover the healing and closure she was so desperate to find.

Your perspective is not everything but it's something. Don't dismiss yourself before you even take a look at what life looks like through your own lens.

If you don't feel like some big hero in your story, welcome to the club. Heroes in literature also feel helpless and lost. They also don't know what the hell to do. They also need help along the way, to shift their perspective and to open their eyes and to mourn the things they still don't know how they lost. Heroes get stuck, they feel self-critical, they draw the wrong conclusions *all the time*. Think of a hero walking into that dark hallway while the audience is screaming, "Noooooo!" Heroes don't see things clearly. This is why we love them—because we recognize we *are* them.

Sometimes being heroic looks like letting go of the notion that you could ever save anyone. Sometimes it looks like surrendering and grieving and giving up and letting go. Heroes aren't always "heroic" in the traditional sense of the word. But when you see yourself as the hero of the story, you stop giving your power away. You finally see yourself for exactly who you are: The one who wants something you can't (yet) have. The one who transforms in some significant way. The one who makes meaning out of it all.

WHAT WE NEED TO KNOW ABOUT THE HERO

There are three simple questions we need to ask about the hero in order to build a story:

1. Who is the hero?
2. What does the hero want (that he or she can't yet have)?
3. How does the hero transform?

We've already established that *you* are the hero. And in Chapter 4, we wrote a word or short phrase that describes the hero at the beginning of the story—a washed-up athlete or a broke single mom. But before we move on to other aspects of the hero, there's one more thing I want you to think about: your hero's backstory.

When I say "backstory," I don't mean that we need to know thirty or forty years of history about your hero. We don't. What I mean is that we may need to know three to five pieces of information about where the hero comes from in order to understand why and how they found themselves in their current predicament.

For example, if your character is a washed-up athlete, it's helpful to know that he attended a top-rated military academy, that he was a first-round draft pick for the Minnesota Vikings, that he was ostracized by his peers for going to the NFL while so many of them went to war, that he warmed the bench for years before getting to play, and that when he finally did get to play, he injured himself in his very first season.

It could also be helpful to know that this young man never had a relationship with his father. He knew very little about his dad except one thing: his dad loved football. So this athlete spent his whole life trying to impress his dad from a distance.

Now that his athletic career is over, he's wondering: *Who am I if I'm not an athlete? What is life without football?*

The information I gave you about this made-up hero is enough for you to understand the predicament he had found himself in. If I'm your reader, I don't need a lengthy history; I don't need every story about what it was like for this young man growing up. All I need is a simple backstory to understand why being an athlete was so important to him and why being *without* sports made this man feel so stuck.

At one of our Write Your Story workshops, we hosted a young woman named Jenn. Jenn described herself at the beginning of her story as a terrified little girl in a woman's body—a forty-year-old woman who didn't even know how to shop for a car. When you read her backstory, you understand why. She grew up in a cult, isolated from the wider world for most of her life, and was threatened that if she abandoned her family and their beliefs, she'd go to hell.

Jenn doesn't need to share every detail about her backstory to help the reader make sense of her present-day plight. Just those few details she shared reiterate her point: a lack of control over her life rendered her terrified to make decisions for herself.

What part of your hero's backstory helps the reader understand the current predicament he or she is in?

WHAT THE HERO WANTS

Now that we know who the hero is and what he or she is *like* at the beginning of the story, we can focus on what the hero *wants* that she can't yet have. What the hero wants helps set the arc for the story because, as you may remember, the story goes where the hero goes. Like a ball thrown across the room.

If the hero wants to fall in love, we'll know the story is over when she stands with her love interest at the top of the Empire State Building. If the hero wants to run a marathon, we won't tune out until she crosses the finish line. If the hero wants to hit $5 million in business, we'll keep trying to "solve" her problems until she finally reaches that threshold. Until that climactic scene arrives, the story isn't over.

Do heroes always get what they set out to achieve? Not exactly. Heroes can realize along the way that they didn't want what they thought they wanted in the first place. They can have a paradigm shift so profound that, by the end of the story, their original pursuit seems pointless. They can also shift so dramatically as a person that what seemed out of reach now seems easily attainable.

No matter what your hero wants, that "want" will help you write the story if you can be as specific as possible.

- Rather than "She wants inner peace," how about "She wants to forgive her dad and have a healthy relationship with her husband."
- Rather than "He wants to feel strong," how about "He wants to win the CrossFit challenge in his region so he can show himself how strong he is."
- Rather than "She wants to be an actress," how about "She wants to win the role in this specific movie."

Here is another instance where it might be helpful to imagine that your story is going to play out on a movie screen. This mental exercise is useful to help you paint a clearer picture. It's hard for "wants to feel confident" to show up on a screen. But you can show a woman walking into an audition where the stakes are high and the pressure is on and it's clear that *everything* is riding on this one performance.

What about your story? What does your hero want that he or she hasn't been able to attain just yet?

- Win the heart of the girl?
- Get that job?
- Run a marathon?
- Have a baby?

- Win the lottery?
- Publish a book?
- Reconnect with a loved one?

If you can't think of a physical, tangible thing you were after in your story, consider how this movie-screen exercise might change your approach to your story altogether.

Remember Grant and his anxiety? When asked what his hero wanted, his answer was, "To stop feeling anxious." But "stop feeling anxious" is more the absence of a thing than an actual thing. It's not specific or visual enough. And even though that *is* for sure what the hero was after, Grant needed a tangible resolution to match his now-tangible problem (panic attacks).

I asked Grant if he could paint a picture for me by imagining his story on a movie screen. I asked him what it would look like if he wasn't wrapped up in his anxious thoughts and if the panic attacks had stopped happening.

Grant thought about it for a minute and then described a scene where he was playing baseball with his nine-year-old son. He was totally present, for over an hour, with no thoughts of what was going on at work, no stress about finances, and no worrying that he "should" be somewhere else. He was able to laugh, play, and be free.

What Grant *wanted* wasn't to stop feeling anxious. He wanted to play baseball with his son without worrying about what was going on elsewhere. He wanted to be free. He wanted to laugh and feel like a kid again.

What about you? What did you want that you couldn't have at the beginning of your story?

HOW DOES YOUR HERO TRANSFORM?

Gil came to one of our first workshops with full confidence in what he wanted. He wanted to win back his wife. In fact, he was on a year-long mission to do it. He admitted that he'd been a terrible husband for nearly a decade. He was addicted to his work and was rarely ever home. He didn't blame his wife for finally getting fed up and leaving.

Since then, he'd had an awakening. He was now on a mission to prove how much he loved her so she would come home.

Gil detailed all the ways he was working on himself. He was in therapy, he'd gone to a meditation retreat in India, he'd sold more than one business, and he would hide his phone from himself for hours at a time. Even his attendance at the Write Your Story workshop was part of this year-long mission to become a better man.

He called it his MBA in emotional maturity.

The only problem was his wife wasn't paying any attention. If anything, she was becoming even more adamant that she wanted a divorce. This devastated Gil but also fueled his resolve to get her back. He kept telling us all weekend that he wasn't going to rest until his wife was back at home.

As the weekend evolved, we fell in love with Gil. His enthusiasm was contagious, and he had a way of seeing the gift in everybody else's story. Every relationship has its own dynamics, and Gil was fully ready to admit fault for not showing up in his marriage the way he knew he should have. But since we loved Gil and were watching him prostrate himself to get his wife's attention, we all had to ask the obvious question: What if, after all of this, she still doesn't change her mind?

This is where writing personal stories can get tricky, and also where it can powerfully shift our perspective. Because it's not only a question about how to write an interesting story. It's also a question about how to direct your life.

At some point, the question the story was asking will get answered. Either Gil's wife will come back or she won't. As narrators (and heroes) of stories, we don't get to choose what other people do inside the story. We only get to choose what *we* do. We get to choose where *we* take the story next.

In a fictional story, the hero can finish first in the marathon or finish last or finish somewhere in between. The narrator gets to choose (and the narrator always chooses the more interesting story). But in a nonfiction story, whether the hero gets the job or wins the race or convinces his wife to come back . . . these endings aren't fully up to the writer.

What *is* up to the writer is how the hero changes inside the circumstances. Here are some ways Gil can transform, even if his wife doesn't return to the marriage:

- He realizes how absent and obsessed with work he was and truly becomes a more present, engaged, loving, heart-connected man.
- He learns the only way to truly love someone is to stop trying to control them, and he releases his wife to do whatever brings her the most peace in her life (even if it causes him great pain).
- He discovers how wonderful he is and how lucky someone would be to have him as a partner.

The hero may not get exactly what he set out to achieve. But when he doesn't, he transforms into a different person who wants different things.

The hero may not get exactly what he set out to achieve. But when he doesn't, he transforms into a different person who wants different things.

If you are a hero who wants something you don't already have—a certain title or a measure of financial success or forgiveness from a loved one or to play baseball with your son—the story might be about getting that thing. It also might be about who you become when you don't get it. And as annoying as this is, many times it's the letting go of what you *thought* you wanted that allows it to finally come to you.

You thought your story was all about healing from cancer or having a baby or overcoming childhood trauma once and for all. What if it was more about *who you became* on the journey to achieve those things?

Taking up the position of the hero is not an arrogant move but an empowered one. It says that although you don't control all the details of your story, you do get to decide where the story is going. No matter what anyone else does or doesn't do, your story is going somewhere spectacular.

No matter what anyone else does or doesn't do, your story is going somewhere spectacular.

You now know who your hero was at the beginning of your story, what they wanted that they didn't have, and who they hope to become by the end of the story. But there's a problem. One Big Problem. And that problem has a specific purpose: it will transport your hero into a whole new world.

CHAPTER 6

Building Tension
(The One Big Problem)

Problems are an essential ingredient to stories. Stories start with problems and are filled with a plethora of problems along the way, and when the problems in the story finally *do* get resolved, the story is over. Problems are what create all the drama and the tension in stories. But problems are about more than just tension. Problems are also the portal the hero walks through in order to get to a brand-new world.

Problems are to stories what gravity is to resistance training. If you're going to use your body weight to get stronger, you need some kind of X factor to enter the equation since just walking around with your regular body weight doesn't produce instant fitness (which is a bummer). When you do a push-up, you push your body weight against the X factor of gravity and voilà—a change takes place. Not instantly, but over time, you gain some pectorals.

The same is true in stories. Without any resistance, the hero of the story won't have any motivation or occasion to change. Why get sober if your current drinking habits are working for you? Why leave your job when you love your coworkers and your boss? Why become humbler when waving your ego around is getting you exactly what you want? Problems enter the story as the X factor the hero pushes against. Problems create resistance, and that resistance engenders change.

Problems are also the portal the hero walks through in order to get to a brand-new world.

Let's face it, we are faced with innumerable "problems" on any given day (for example, my one-year-old son filled several pairs of my shoes with water in the bathtub this morning while I was making breakfast, which was a new problem I had yet to face). But the question isn't just, What are my problems? The question is, What are my problems as they relate to getting what I want in the story? Clear problems are much easier to identify once we know what the hero wants that he or she can't have.

When you think about what you're after inside the story you are writing, what is getting in the way of reaching your objective? Take a minute to think about what problems you might be facing inside your own story. Consider these examples:

- You want to feel free, but you have anxiety (and keep having panic attacks).
- You want to start a business, but you don't have the capital (all you have is five dollars).
- You feel called to write a book, but you don't know the first thing about publishing.
- You are desperate to fall in love, but online dating sucks the life out of you (and you can't forget when that guy even tried to take you to a strip club on your first date).
- You vowed to be a great mother, but you keep losing your temper (which your own mother used to do)
- You are ready to quit drinking, but you can't imagine your life without alcohol.
- You want to believe in God, but you can no longer continue with the faith of your childhood.
- You would love to live in community, but you have no friends.

What is the problem that is keeping you from your desired outcome?

Here's another way writing your story helps you remap your life. What if the problems you face in your life aren't actually the *problems* you think they are? Problems build tension. Problems test the hero's resolve. Problems draw out the hero's best qualities. Problems make the hero *think* about turning back—until she remembers why she was on this journey in the first place. Problems bring the hero back to her *why* and deepen her commitment. Problems are the X factor ushering in the resolution.

Without problems, what are you pushing against?

Imagine a story about a woman who goes through a divorce but doesn't feel any pain in the process. She isn't confused about what to do. She doesn't question her own sanity. She isn't heartbroken. She just wakes up one day, decides to get a divorce, and goes down to the lawyer's office to sign the papers. It would be a short (and boring) story.

Now imagine a story about a hero who wants a certain high-paying job? He sends in his resume, has the interview, and gets the job on the spot. No waiting. No obstacles. No problem to overcome. If it happened in real life, wonderful. But I doubt you'd feel compelled to write it down.

Watch what happens, though, when I throw some problems in the hero's path. What if we have a hero who wants to get a certain high-paying job, but he's not sure he has the chops to live up to the job title? Forget his resume, which is woefully lacking. He hardly has the self-confidence to apply for the job, let alone fight for it through a rigorous interview process. He knows the guys he'll be up against— and they're jerks. They bullied him from elementary school all the way through law school.

Just when he's about to give up on applying at all, he gets an email from his high school crush, asking if he'll be at the reunion in a couple of months. He imagines what it would be like to show up, dressed to impress, with his new job title and see his dream girl for the first time in ten years.

See how the tension in the story is ramping up thanks to problems? The hero now has something to push against. He now has the motivation to act, to make a change.

I'm being playful here. This story reads more like a romantic comedy than it does a real-life story. But what I want you to see is how adding more problems to the hero's plate actually makes us root for him even more.

What if we send him to his parents' house, where his mom patronizes him and his dad criticizes him? What if we put him at the gym (he's trying to get fit for the reunion), and he can't even lift the bench press bar itself, let alone put any weight on it? What if his computer, with his bare-bones resume on it, crashes so he has to start again from scratch?

The more problems the hero faces, the more interesting the story becomes, the more believable it is, the more we resonate with the hero and feel that he is "like us," and the more we cheer for his eventual success. Problems work in stories because we register them as real life.

Obviously, I'm playing with a fictional story here. But think about your real story for a minute. What problems have you faced on the journey to achieving what you want? If you have faced a host of problems—and most of us have—consider how this might actually be *good* for you and your story. How might these problems be showing you the way? How might they be drawing out your strengths? How might these problems be the very X factor you need in order to change? In stories and in life, problems do a number of things for you:

- They create tension, which keeps you engaged.
- They build trust with the reader that the hero is "like them."
- They enlist the support of others who are rooting for the hero to change.
- They challenge the hero to change in a positive way.
- They show the hero what he or she is made of.
- They ground the story in reality since we recognize that problems are a part of life.
- They build suspense and momentum toward the ending.
- They make the resolution more satisfying.

I'm not suggesting we manufacture fake problems for the sake of telling a more compelling story. I don't have the mindset that life has to be hard in order to be interesting. I *do* have the mindset that problems are inevitable, that you're bound to encounter them, and that when they show up in your life and in your story, it might help you to think of them as an X factor you're pushing against so you can grow.

In fact, playing with a structure like storytelling can reveal to you how small your problems are in the grand scheme of things. How, despite the existence of problems inside a story, the hero always—*always*—finds a way to overcome them. If your problems aren't solved, it simply means your story isn't over.

If your problems aren't solved, it
simply means your story isn't over.

Problems are portals that usher the hero of a story into a new reality.

THE ONE BIG PROBLEM (OBP)

In order to solve the many problems life throws our way, we need to focus on one specific problem at a time. I call this the One Big Problem (OBP).

Imagine you were trying to solve a financial crisis and a relationship crisis and a health crisis all at the same time. (Maybe you don't need to imagine.) Or perhaps you've faced some other cocktail-of-life crises all mixed up into the same season. If that's the case, you know that in order to make progress on any of the problems you face, you need to do one of two things:

1. **Focus on only *one* of the multiple problems**. For example, perhaps you realize that until you

solve your health crisis, none of the other crises even matter. So you choose to start with the OBP of your health so that you can eventually face the other problems.

2. **Realize the "larger" problem at play.** Maybe when you zoom out, you are able to realize that your multiple problems are all part of one "bigger" problem. For example, maybe you're able to see that you keep saying yes when you mean to say no, and *that's* the OBP that needs a solution. Once that problem gets solved, it will naturally solve the other sub-problems.

Either way, this is about simplifying many problems down to One Big Problem so that you have more clarity about where the story is trying to go. When you create clarity around problems in a story by zeroing in on the OBP, the hero becomes single-minded and singularly focused on solving *one* issue. With all her energy pointed in one direction, she's able to push off the resistance of that problem and make progress toward her goal.

As much as stories thrive on problems, a story will also suffer if the hero is trying to solve too many disjointed problems at the same time. If the reader can't see how these problems are connected or see a clear path that the hero is trying to follow, the story will get muddled and confusing, and the reader will lose interest.

But again, it's not just the reader who loses interest in the story if there's not one clear problem. It's also the *hero*.

Picture yourself being expected to solve a dozen problems at once without any sense of how they are all connected. You'll either get overwhelmed or just not catch any interest at all.

Imagine a story where the hero has thirty days of overhead left in her business and no new revenue in sight. Also, her mother in law is mad that she didn't bring the family to visit for Christmas this year. Oh, and the hero's dog is sick. And before I forget to mention it, the hero knows she should probably get a colonoscopy because she has a family history of colon cancer.

Before the hero can engage with the story and take action, she has to decide which problem guides the story. Which path is she going to follow? Her OBP might be that she is terrified to speak up for herself and advocate for what she needs. That OBP would, in a way, tie all the disjointed details together. In order to resolve her story, she would need to use her voice and come to her own defense with regard to her business, her mother-in-law, and the medical system to get the tests she needs.

Alternatively, the OBP might be related to the business *only*, and the rest of the details will have to fall away. It's possible that, for this story, the family and health problems aren't relevant. I'm not suggesting they are irrelevant *period*, just that they might be irrelevant within this specific story. All of that depends on how the hero defines her OBP.

If you're not sure how to hone in on your OBP, a good exercise is to go back and check your Controlling Idea.

Your OPB should "match" the obstacle you identified in your Controlling Idea. If it doesn't match, you have two choices: edit your OBP or update your Controlling Idea.

Defining the OBP provides consistency and stability for the hero. There's no question about what the objective is. She knows exactly where to focus her attention. And when she focuses all her attention toward the OBP, it doesn't just make the story more interesting. It makes *her* more likely to become the kind of person who can eventually solve it.

You likely have several problems you're facing inside your own story. Your long list of problems might look like Hannah's did when she first came to our Write Your Story workshop:

- A cheating husband
- Four young kids
- Financial dependence (no reliable income or money set aside)
- Hated the idea of divorce
- Didn't know a good attorney
- Kids love their dad
- Confronted husband and he lied
- Nowhere to live
- Unsupportive family members ("married couples work it out")
- Bitter mistress spreading rumors

The question we need to ask is: What do all these problems have in common? After unpacking her story, I helped

Hannah define her OBP as one question: *Should I stay or should I go?*

Hannah had a dozen or so problems to solve. But what is the *one* problem that connected all these problems together? Hannah had to decide if she was going to stay in this dishonest marriage where she had financial stability and predictability or if she was going to leave her husband and take a leap into the unknown. Unpacking that problem *included* all of the other problems. But that was the OBP she needed to solve.

What about your own story? What is the OBP you need to solve? What is the one thing getting in the way of what the hero is trying to achieve?

SEE IT IN ACTION

When I was pregnant with my daughter, I said what (I assume) most pregnant moms say about giving birth: I wanted to give birth to a happy, healthy baby. As for the rest of the details, I was open. I planned to give birth at a highly rated hospital in our area, to bring a doula with me, and to experience the miracle of childbirth with my husband by my side.

Then COVID happened.

Because of the COVID-19 pandemic and the restrictions in our area, I learned I wouldn't be able to bring a birth doula with me to the hospital, and the chances were high I wouldn't be allowed to have my husband in the room either. Nothing was set in stone, but restrictions were changing on a daily basis, and I didn't want to play roulette, taking a chance with where they would land when I went into labor. My exact words to my husband were, "There's no way in hell I'm giving birth to this baby without you there."

Famous last words.

I started exploring alternative options. I found a birthing center in my neighborhood and decided I'd give birth there instead. That way both my husband and my doula could attend. Problem solved. Except not so much.

When I went into labor, my contractions came on fast, and I could tell something was wrong. I raced to the birth center. A midwife took my blood pressure and shook her head. I'd need to go straight to the hospital. "Possible preeclampsia," I heard her say to my husband as we walked out the door. I'd heard that word only one other time in my life—on a TV episode where the mother died in childbirth.

Needless to say, when we arrived at the hospital, I was in rough shape. That's when I learned that they weren't going to let my husband come with me to the delivery room. In order to join me, he would need to pass a health inspection, and I would need to be "officially admitted" to the hospital.

"Officially admitted?" I screamed at the poor orderly who was wheeling me into labor and delivery. "What are you planning on doing—sending me home?!"

I could go on and on for *pages* with problems from this story:

- My cell phone died trying to FaceTime Matt, who was waiting outside (literally outside the doors of the hospital, as he wasn't even allowed in the waiting room).
- My daughter's heart rate dropped during the delivery.
- Nella wasn't breathing when she was born and had to be rushed to the NICU, as I shared in Chapter 3.
- Hospital staff wouldn't allow me see my daughter in the NICU until my blood pressure came down.
- I wasn't allowed to eat any solid foods because of the medication I was taking.

Problems upon problems. And yet as many problems as I faced, they were all the result of my One *Big* Problem, which is that I was giving birth in the midst of a global pandemic. That was my OBP.

By the way, I only shared the *problems* I faced in this particular story, but do you see the beginning of a narrative arc forming here? This is a story about a pregnant woman who wants to give birth in a peaceful way, with her husband by her side, but when she faces a childbirth she never expected, she discovers a peace and support that passes logical understanding.

MAKING THE PROBLEM "REAL"

Sometimes the problem we *think* is the problem is not actually the problem. Sometimes the most accurate, most specific problem in the story is outside of our current awareness. In this case, the problem doesn't become clear until you write it down.

This process of writing your story will often raise your awareness so that you "see" your problem for the first time.

Think about this for a second. If you really knew what your OBP was—if you had clearly honed in on it—don't you think you would have solved it already? Problems don't always get solved right away, but they sure get solved a lot faster when we clearly understand what the *real* problem is.

Problems don't always get solved right away, but they sure get solved a lot faster when we clearly understand what the real problem is.

As a simple example, my three-year-old just came to me to tell me her stomach hurts. That is a problem, yes. But since I happen to know that she ate two little bags of gummy bears before eating her breakfast, I have the awareness that her problem is not really a tummy ache. It's too much sugar on an empty stomach. (Or is her problem that she has parents who let her eat gummy bears before breakfast?) Only *you* get to define what your OBP is, but the more specific and accurate you can be, the more interesting your story will be. And the more likely you are to actually solve your problem!

One way to make your problem more specific is to define it beyond a feeling. Notice how the silly problem I shared above wasn't just about a tummy ache. It was about gummy bears. Gummy bears are more tangible than a tummy ache. I can picture them and even hold them in my hand. Tangibility is a helpful tool inside storytelling. What are the "gummy bears" to your "tummy ache"? Consider these examples:

- Feeling helpless: watching a sick child wither away
- Feeling anxious: being eight days away from filing for bankruptcy
- Feeling grief: losing a spouse three months after your second child is born
- Feeling betrayed: evidence of your husband's mistress

Do you see how making the OBP "real" puts some meat on the bones of the problem? It gives you something you can sink your teeth into.

A reader can't always "grab on" to a feeling like helplessness or anxiety. What's much easier to grab on to is a dying father or a sudden job loss or a mugging in a park. You might think that being this specific would alienate a reader who doesn't share your experience, but the opposite is actually true. The universals are found *inside* the specifics.

If the OBP you faced in your story was something like "being lost," ask yourself how you can translate that into a real problem. How did feeling lost show up in your life? Was it a drug problem? Depression? Sitting around all day watching Netflix? Were there physical symptoms, like a loss of appetite or an illness of some kind?

Notice how I take some examples from this book and identify an OBP.

- Clark wants to play baseball with his son, but he **keeps having panic attacks**.
- Svetka wants to learn more about her history, but her **mother is quickly dying**.
- Gil wants to win his wife back, but she's **filing for divorce**.

Notice how the problems I listed in the stories above are "real" problems. You can picture seeing them on a movie screen. The fact that they have this tangible nature will make the problems easier to write about and easier to solve, and they make for a more interesting story.

Take a minute and think about your story and what you already know. You know what your story is about (the Controlling Idea). You know what makes your story interesting and where you want to enter the action (the Opening Line). You've defined who your hero is at the beginning of the story and what he or she wants, and you've even considered how that person might transform by the end of the story.

Inside that structure, what is the OBP the hero had to face in order to reach a resolution?

AMPLIFY THE PROBLEM

If making your problem "real" feels like a stretch for you, you'll enjoy this next step. Once you identify the tangible problem your hero is facing, you can *amplify* that problem by revealing the inner environment of the hero. Think about the external experience the hero faced—the divorce or the hiking trip or the loss of a mother at a young age— and ask yourself how this made the hero *feel*.

This is where you can move from problems that show up on a movie screen to more emotional or philosophical ones.

- She's scared.
- He's insecure.
- She has imposter syndrome.
- He has unresolved anger.
- She doesn't know if she has what it takes.

While the reader might "get" that panic attacks are a big problem, she gets it even more when she reads Grant's internal dialogue. When she discovers that Grant questions his own sanity, that he worries he might not have what it takes to be a good husband and father, and that he worries everyone he loves would leave him if they only knew the truth, she *now* understands more deeply why these panic attacks are the OBP that they are. The inner environment amplifies the tension.

The hero's backstory could come into play again here too.

You might already be invested in the story, knowing that Hannah has a cheating husband and four young children to think about. But you become *more* invested when you learn that she has a controlling father who made her question her own judgment and that years with a gaslighting husband made her second-guess her sanity. When you understand her backstory and her internal environment, the OBP she's facing seems like an even *bigger* problem.

When you "amplify" the problem, you help the reader understand why the problem is such a big deal for the hero in the first place. It's one thing to know that Jake wants the job but has an abysmal resume. It's another thing to know that he was bullied incessantly throughout his childhood, always questioned his own abilities, has a critical father who made him feel terrible about himself, and has decided that he'll never amount to anything.

The more you amplify the tension, the more interesting the story becomes. A clear internal environment secures the reader's support for the hero. He's flawed but lovable. He reminds us of ourselves. We may not know exactly what it feels like to want the job but not get it. But we sure as heck know what it feels like to question our own abilities. We know what it feels like to allow that insecurity to keep us from moving forward.

Beyond reader support, the tension the OBP problem creates is the main ingredient of heroic change. It's the X factor that we heroes push against. The more tension present in the story, the more opportunity for growth, the bigger our metaphorical pectorals become, and the more we get to see what we're made of. And what we are made of is more miraculous than we could have ever imagined.

HOW THE HERO SURVIVES

The hero is up against her One Big Problem, dozens of smaller problems inside the big problem, an inner environment of problems, and even a host of unresolved past problems (backstory) that are being pulled to the forefront from this experience. How in the world will she ever be able to overcome the obstacles she faces? How will she find the strength? It seems impossible. And it very well might be.

That is, until she meets her guide.

CHAPTER 7

Help for the Hero
(The Guide)

At this point in the story, the hero is in need of some serious help. She is up against a problem she cannot solve on her own (the OBP). We know she can't solve it, because if she could, she would have done it already. If she had the wisdom or resolve to solve this problem, we wouldn't be reading (or writing) this story.

Not only that, but this OBP is causing a whole host of other problems. It's making her question herself and her sanity, and it's bringing up memories of other times she wasn't able to solve problems in the past.

She needs someone to enter the story and give her a push, some encouragement, some perspective.

That's where the guide comes in.

I find the guide to be a favorite part of the framework for most writers because the guide helps the rest of the story begin to make sense. The hero is up against an impossible wall. How will he get to the other side? The guide. That's how. The guide shifts the hero's perspective, offers support, suggests a new way forward, and generally "saves" the hero from what would otherwise have been certain failure.

The guide doesn't solve the problem *for* the hero. That wouldn't make for a very satisfying story. We need to see the hero achieve the successful result for himself. The guide simply shifts the hero's perspective *so that* the hero can see things more clearly. So that the hero can solve the problem in his or her own way.

If the hero doubts herself, the guide helps her find her inner strength and wisdom. If the hero has "tried everything," the guide suggests something (maybe even something obvious) that the hero hasn't yet tried. If the hero is scared, the guide might push her into the very thing that scares her. The guide reminds the hero what's important, points her to her inner strength and resolve, and helps her become the hero she wants to be.

Guides are lovely, inspiring, endearing characters in our stories, and it's a special feeling to get to write them in. As we explore this part of the framework, our eyes are often opened to the many people who have supported us along the way. We might have thought we were alone in our struggle, but no. We were *guided*. And as we define who it was who directed us and what we learned from them, their wisdom becomes illuminated in a new way.

We might have thought we were alone in our struggle, but no. We were guided.

The guide was always there before, but we didn't always see her for the gift she was. Now we do. We understand how the wisdom of the guide allowed us to find our way.

WHO IS MY GUIDE?

When you think of the word *guide*, you probably imagine some wise, sage character who is an expert in one way or another. Guides can certainly look like this. But guides can also come in unexpected packages. Guides can be younger than the hero or lower in status in some way. In a chapter of *Indestructible*, I skip church and meet a guide—an older woman who has had a few too many glasses of wine on a Sunday morning—at a bar.

She tells me that, if she were my mom, she would be proud of me. And it's that passing comment that allows me to release the assumption I've been holding on to: that I must be a disappointment to my parents.

A guide doesn't have to be someone you know, and you don't have to have a personal relationship with them. Your guide can be an author, a speaker, a radio personality, a relative who isn't living (like in the case of Svetka's letters from her grandmother), or even God, whatever your conception of God is.

The guide is a character who helps the hero change her mind about something in her story so she can make progress.

- Jack wants to start his own business but doesn't even have a high school diploma, so he holds back, fearing he doesn't have what it takes. His father, Ed (the guide), suggests, "Maybe you're overestimating what it takes to start."

- Grace wants to get married but is waiting for the "right guy" to show up in her life. Her best friend, Mel (the guide), says, "What do you think? He's just going to show up on your doorstep?"

- Walter is fired as CEO after giving twenty years of his life to his company. On the drive home, he questions everything he thought was true and considers making himself disappear. He exits the freeway in an unfamiliar place and turns onto an unknown road, and that's when he sees it: a yard sign (the guide) that reads, "YOU MATTER."

- Uma wants to reform healthcare, but she's up against some of the richest and most powerful conglomerates in the world. Just when she's about to give up, her sister (the guide) tells her, "They might have the money, Uma. But you have something they don't have." And she points to her sister's heart.

- Lorenzo is a high school graduate who wants to do
something significant with his life but isn't sure what
he's passionate about. All the advice given to him
from parents and friends just seems to fall flat. Then
one day as he's driving, he hears a voice on a podcast (the guide) share about an opportunity to travel
around the world learning to river raft. He can't
explain why, but he just *knows* he's supposed to go.

As you think about who your guide might be and how
they might have shifted your thinking or offered you a new
way forward, here is a basic framework to keep in mind:

1.   Hero is stuck behind a problem (OBP)
2.   Guide enters the story and makes a suggestion
("Have you thought about it this way . . . ?")
3.   Hero acts differently from how he or she has acted
before and *finally* makes progress

The guide is the tipping point. If you felt uncomfortable putting yourself in the middle of your story as the
hero, you'll enjoy this part. This helps it all make sense. You
couldn't have shifted without your guide. You couldn't have
possibly overcome your problem without them. (If you could
have, you would have done it already.) Without the guide's
ever-important redirection, you'd still be stuck behind your
One Big Problem.

What would we do without our guides?

HOW THE GUIDE HELPS THE HERO

People often want to know if there can be more than one guide in a story, and the simple answer is yes. In personal stories there is *often* more than one guide. In a story as short as yours (three to five pages), however, let's focus on identifying at least *one* guide in the story and qualifying exactly how that guide helps you to change.

Guides help heroes evolve by offering a different way of thinking, a new idea, or a paradigm shift that the hero hasn't considered before.

Guides help heroes evolve by offering a different way of thinking, a new idea, or a paradigm shift that the hero hasn't considered before.

Take a minute and think about how naturally this happens in real life. Let's say you're in a conflict with a coworker, for example. You're frustrated and confused about why this coworker would treat you the way they do. You try to speak up for yourself on a few different occasions but end up getting even more tangled up in a toxic relationship with this person. You're at a loss for what to do.

So you tell the story to your best friend (the guide), who, as a happy bonus, is a therapist and always has important insights into workplace conflicts.

Sure enough, your best friend asks you a handful of questions and then makes an important point: "Stop expecting people to act different from the way they've acted *every time* before."

You're stunned. It is so simple.

"Maybe your frustration," your friend suggests, "is that you're expecting this person to be something they cannot be."

You go back to work the next day with better boundaries and a new expectation, and voilà, your coworker may still be acting crazy, but you're not as triggered.

Or how about this situation?

You're driving to work one morning when some insane driver cuts across four lanes of traffic to get to his exit. You have to swerve to miss him, and he nearly causes a multicar pileup. Incensed, you wave your arms and yell at the driver to slow down or he's going to kill someone.

Then you remember something your mom (the guide) used to say to you about how you never know what someone is going through behind the scenes. "They might seem like selfish jerks on the surface," she'd say about your middle school bullies. "But maybe their parents don't love them as much as I love you." Then she'd lean in and give you a kiss on your forehead.

Suddenly, your heart softens and you wish the crazy driver well, hoping he (and everyone else on the road) safely gets to wherever he needs to go.

Do you see how the guide works to shift and transform the hero?

One last example just to drive this point home: Let's say your story is about trying to "right the ship" of culture at the company you founded, which, despite your best efforts, has become ultracompetitive and toxic. As the hero of the story, you're still trying to figure out the role you play in all of this.

How much of this did I create? you wonder. *And who from my team needs to go?*

To get the answers you need, you begin consulting your guides. Here's a great example of how multiple guides might make sense. You call your best friend, who works in another industry but is also an entrepreneur. You ask your wife, who knows you better than anyone. You call your mentor, a man who is a couple decades older than you, who sold his business and retired. And you ask your therapist about it during your next scheduled meeting.

Your wife suggests that if you want your employees to act in a more collaborative way, you are going to need to lead by example. She reminds you of a deal you did recently where you ultimately got what you wanted, but you had to step ever so slightly out of your character in order to achieve it.

"What if you were honest with your employees about that? What if you shared a small piece of your regret?"

Your best friend suggests two employees from your team who have to go, as soon as possible. "I've known they were a problem since I met them two years ago," he says.

Your mentor offers a framework you can use to encourage relationship and collaboration on the team. He used it at his company, which year over year was voted one of the best places to work.

Your therapist flips the question back on you: "What do *you* think needs to be done?" In other words, Why are you relying so much on guidance *outside* of yourself but ignoring your own inner guidance?

How this man chooses to move forward will determine how his story unfolds. But do you notice how his guides lead the way? If he chooses to ignore his guides, his story will fall flat and he'll go back to what has always been. But if he listens to them and takes their advice to heart, he can't help but shift the course of his story forever.

THE PARADIGM SHIFT

Now that you're beginning to see who your guide might be, I want to help you define exactly how this person shifted your perspective. This will help you determine what's called a paradigm shift, a key element in understanding your guide and your story. A paradigm shift is a shift in perspective that helps your hero think, feel, or act differently than they were thinking, feeling, or acting before they met the guide. It's this shift that leads them to a new outcome.

To understand the paradigm shift your guide offers, ask yourself:

How does the guide help the hero think, feel, or act differently?

I find the easiest way to define the paradigm shift is to define the "before" and "after" first, and then determine what the insight was that caused the shift. The before and after shift might look something like this:

I used to think _____. But now I think _____.

I used to feel _____. But now I feel _____.

I used to be _____. But now I am _____.

I used to do _____. But now I do _____.

- I used to think that online dating was a miserable experience, but now I know that you can actually find a great relationship online.
- I used to feel unsure of myself when making decisions, but now I go with my gut and don't waste time questioning myself.
- I used to judge others and myself, but now I have more compassion.
- I used to drink twelve cups of coffee per day, but now I only drink two or three.

Once you determine your before and after shift, you can then identify the insight or wisdom that helped you make that shift. How did your guide help you see what you didn't see before? How did they open your mind? How did they help you shift your perspective?

If you have read *Indestructible*, you know that my guide's name in that story was Sarah. Sarah was a yoga instructor with a quirky personality who helped me get out of my head and see my life for the gift it was. One of the things she did over and over inside that story was place one hand on her belly and one hand on her heart and say, "I'm in my life with my whole heart." She would have me mimic her. And by the end of the book, I started to embody that message: *I'm in my life with my whole heart.*

Here's how I would state the paradigm shift:

> **I used to live my life half-heartedly. Now I am in my life with my whole heart.**

It might be helpful to clarify that I never overtly *state* that paradigm shift in the book itself. You won't find it in writing. But understanding the paradigm shift was essential to building the story arc and demonstrating the hero's transformation. The same will be true for you. You may not state your paradigm shift directly, but you do need to identify it and understand its role in the story.

The guides in our lives are pivot points in our story. The hero often puts in a good bit of effort before the guide gets there, but at that point she has run out of resources and ideas. By the time the guide arrives, the hero has "tried everything." It is only the guide's new perspective (the paradigm shift) that allows the hero to see what wasn't available to her before.

The guides are the characters who deserve the credit. The guides are the wise sages who swoop in to save the day. The guides are the ones who have a life-changing perspective. The hero hasn't gotten there yet. But she will.

WHAT IF I DON'T HAVE A GUIDE?

Macy came to a Write Your Story workshop with a story that was hard to stomach, honestly. She had suffered horrific abuse at the hands of her family members and then was betrayed again by a broken legal system, the very system designed to protect her. The courage it took for her to show up and write her story inspired the whole room.

During the "guide" section of the workshop, Macy came to talk to me one-on-one. She was worried she didn't have any guides. The description of the guide, she said, didn't fit anyone in her story. All the people in her story who were supposed to help her had failed. Miserably. In fact, she was *still* in a legal battle to that very day trying to keep her parents and her ex-husband from having access to her daughter.

Macy is not the only writer who has ever worried she doesn't have a guide. One in every handful of writers I work with doesn't immediately see a guide when they look at their story. Especially those folks who have been trained or told—or have for some reason decided that it's best—to do everything themselves.

I reminded Macy that guides can come in unlikely packages and that they aren't always people. They can be animals or angels or lyrics to a song we hear on the radio. Guides can show up in the form of repeated messages, like seeing the same phrase written, or the same color, or the same time on the clock over and over again.

I asked Macy how she'd survived all that she survived. You don't go through something as horrific as what she faced and then just wake up one day and decide you want to write your story. To gather the courage Macy had, I knew she had to know how much she mattered. That *her* story was part of a larger narrative.

"How did you get here?" I wondered.

Macy thought about it for a moment. "Books," she said. "I would disappear into the world of my books and for a short period of time, the pain would vanish. Sometimes I think the only reason I'm alive is because of books."

Those authors and characters, I told her, are your guides.

Guides are everywhere if you're willing to see them. Your perception of the world and of the life you are living can always be shifted if you are open to it. You don't need a mentor or a coach to help you see (although sometimes you get one of those, and it's wonderful). You might have the number 8 that shows up everywhere you go, the vivid dreams where your mother comes to visit, the cardinal that perches at your back window, or the sound of the wind in the trees. You are guided. You are supported. Your story is leading you.

Guides are everywhere if you're willing to see them.

I suppose this is another way you heal when you write your story. You begin to see that nothing is fixed, no problem is insurmountable, no story is fully written, and you are not alone in any of it. We are ever-evolving, complicated creatures, who sometimes are up against impossible problems. And sometimes impossible problems dissolve when we find a slightly different way to see them.

I had a therapist many years ago who would tell me, "There are many ways in which to see a thing." I was having a hard time making sense of my life at the time, and she would remind me over and over, "Make sure you walk all the way around this issue a couple of times. Don't land on anything until you see it from a few different angles."

Writing our stories helps us see an event in our life from a few different angles. It helps us to shift our perspective, to uncover a detail that was always there but that we never noticed before, to witness ourselves in our struggle, and to fully receive the wisdom that our guides have to offer. When we do that, something truly miraculous happens.

We *too* become the guides.

When you understand your own story, it doesn't just become a lamppost for you. It becomes a beacon for others too. Your story *itself* is a guide. It is leading you and those who are watching you down a path to inevitable resolution.

CHAPTER 8

The Path to Resolution (The Struggle and Relief)

Whatever it was you were after at the beginning of your story, chances are you didn't try one strategy and immediately achieve your successful outcome.

If you were hoping to launch a new business, you didn't come out of the gates with a lucrative launch on your first try. Or, if you did, you wouldn't be writing the story. The stories we feel compelled to write—and the ones we love to read—are the ones where the hero struggles for a long time before *finally* finding their way to resolution.

In the story you're writing, I'm willing to bet you tried a whole host of strategies to get what you were after. You likely exhausted all your resources but nothing worked. Then you tried something *really* out-of-the-box, but that didn't seem to help either. Finally, you met someone (the guide) who helped you shift your perspective, or your approach, and finally, finally, when it seemed like all was lost, you had a breakthrough.

That's how stories work.

You'll find that pattern present in your life quite often too.

I read recently that it takes four hundred attempts at something new for your brain to create a new synapse. That rings true. Your brain is literally carving a new path, creating a road where there wasn't one before. Imagine yourself plodding a trail through a dense forest. You'd expect that process to take some time. You'd have to put in some reps. You'd need to be willing to trace that same trajectory a few hundred times.

The stories we feel compelled to write—and the ones we love to read—are the ones where the hero struggles for a long time before finally finding their way to resolution.

The same is true for stories. When a hero gets stuck in a rut, he rarely gets out in one attempt. And while there's no rule of thumb for the number of attempts a hero has to make, four hundred feels about right. (I'm being cheeky. Four hundred would be a long story. Let's shoot for three to five.)

Take a minute to think about your hero and what she wanted that she didn't have at the beginning of the story. What "road" did she have to walk in order to get to where she was going? What happened on the journey? How many reps did it take? What trials and failures did she have to go through before she reached her hopeful resolution?

You might start by simply listing what happened in the story:

1. Hero gets a terrifying diagnosis.
2. Hero goes home to calm down but tells no one.
3. Hero reaches out for a second opinion and a third and a fourth and a fifth . . .
4. Hero decides she is unsatisfied with all the opinions and goes searching for an alternative path to healing.
5. Hero finds another method but that method fails.
6. Hero meets a guide who suggests an even more obscure method and that attempt succeeds!
7. Hero finds healing.

The Struggle and Relief that guides all stories to resolution is present right here, in this list of simply what took place. Each little stone along the path has *some* struggle and *some* relief. There's a small "arc" present inside each little brick.

It might be helpful to think of this part of the story as the "road" your hero walks to get from "the hero who wants something" to "the resolution." Many different events will take place in this section of the story. It might take up the bulk of your three to five pages of writing. Some of what occurs will challenge the hero, even break him. Others will provide the hero with small, necessary moments of relief.

Consider the path you've walked inside your own story. What has taken place? What events have unfolded? What details need to be included in the story for the reader to understand the journey? Some of these events have challenged you, pushed you, stretched you, broken you, or provided you with necessary resistance.

Some of these events have brought you some relief.

THE RELIEF

When you hear me say *relief*, don't take this to mean total relief. In fact, if there is ever a point of total relief inside your story, it's the end of the story. Instead, think of what happens to a pressure cooker if you let just a little bit of the steam out at a time. That's what you want to do with your Struggle and Relief. You want to let out just enough steam so that nothing explodes, but you also want to keep some tension so the story keeps "cooking."

Relief could be things like

- Finally admitting something to yourself
- Shedding a few tears
- Discovering an important truth (that perhaps introduces new problems)
- Taking action that is necessary for the evolution of the story but also scares you
- Apologizing to someone for something you did

- Quitting something (a job, an addiction, a habit)
- Making that phone call you've been putting off
- Learning a new piece of information
- Having a small "success" with something you try
- Seeing a glimmer of hope on the horizon
- Laughing at how funny the problem or obstacles is

As we already discussed, the *struggle* serves the larger story by building tension and intrigue. The *relief* contributes by offering the reminder that we *are* moving down the path toward eventual success. Without these small moments of relief in your life story, you might give up on the story altogether—and so might your reader! But when we let out a little "steam" in our story, the pressure continues to build toward a powerful ending.

FUN AND GAMES

I call this section the Struggle and Relief, but the famous screenwriter and teacher Blake Snyder calls it Fun and Games.[6] I appreciate his sense of humor, especially as I apply it to my personal life.

Needless to say, this is the space in your story where you can actually have a lot of fun with the problems that are inevitably present in your story. Sometimes, when dealing with personal problems, we bring a seriousness to the table that is unhelpful to the task of problem-solving. Creativity thrives where there is permission to play. So, as serious as the problems in your story might seem, let's play and see what might arise!

Creativity thrives where there is permission to play.

See if you can bring some "fun and games" to the potentially very serious problems present in your story.

You have already identified the One Big Problem your hero is trying to overcome—addiction, lack of identity, a toxic relationship, etc.—and you've also considered a handful of smaller sub-problems your hero is facing as a result of The One Big Problem.

Problems like . . .

- Not knowing what to do next
- Lack of funds
- Lack of experience
- Toxic roommate
- Unreasonable boss
- Needing a good divorce attorney
- Lacking identity
- Struggling to get out of bed in the morning

A great place for the sub-problems in your story is in the "struggle" part of Struggle and Relief, which will look something like this:

STEP 1: Struggle. Relief.

STEP 2: Struggle. Relief.

STEP 3: Struggle. Relief.

STEP 4: Struggle. Relief.

STEP 5: Struggle. Relief.

Let me show you how this works with a fictional story.

Let's imagine that twenty-one-year-old Emily (the hero) is pregnant for the first time and she doesn't know who the father is (the One Big Problem). She's scared and doesn't know how she's going to be a mom when she has zero experience with babies (amplifies the problem). But she really wants to be a good mom—the kind of mom her mother wasn't able to be for her. She wants to change her family's legacy for the better.

Her Struggle and Relief could look something like this:

- **STEP 1**: Takes the pregnancy test scared and alone (struggle). Gets the positive result (relief).
- **STEP 2**: Goes shopping for supplies but has no idea what she's doing (struggle). Leaves the store in tears (relief).
- **STEP 3**: Can't keep any food down (struggle). Eats mac and cheese and falls asleep (relief).
- **STEP 4**: Calls her mother to break the news (struggle). Her mother celebrates the news (relief).

- **STEP 5**: Goes to her first OB appointment alone (struggle). Sees the sonogram picture and cries (relief).

Once you see this play out in a story, you realize how it is not only effective at keeping a reader's attention, but it also is a pattern that teaches you to look for the moments of relief that are inevitably present in your story. Lots of problems. Just as many solutions.

Creating your own Struggle and Relief can feel like a bit of a game because it does challenge you to look for "relief" where you might not have seen it before. Relief doesn't mean resolved. If the hero's problems were *resolved*, the story would be over. Where did you find some small amount of relief from each sub-problem on the long road to your eventual resolution?

WHY STRUGGLE AND RELIEF?

From a narrative perspective, the purpose of the Struggle and Relief is to build tension so that the reader will continue to pay attention. Remember that when the problems go away, the story goes away. When the tension is gone, the interest is gone. So you have to keep reminding your reader that the story isn't over. There are still more problems to be resolved.

But on a psychological level, Struggle and Relief has to exist because we recognize that this is how the hero changes. If the hero is going to become the person we know he can be, he or she must face (and overcome) some big challenges. He needs some *resistance* to grow those pecs.

Imagine a story where the hero transformed from a self-involved and power-hungry leader to a compassionate and inclusive one without really going through some hardships along the way. We wouldn't believe the story was real. Transformation doesn't happen like that. Change happens when life *forces* us to change by throwing some difficulties in our path.

Change happens when life forces us to change by throwing some difficulties in our path.

The Struggle and Relief is how the hero gets physically stronger in some cases, but also how he becomes emotionally and psychologically stronger. It's this set of experiences that teaches the hero the lessons she needs to learn in order to overcome her One Big Problem. The Struggle and Relief builds her into a woman who has the chops to finally stand on that stage or to set a boundary or take down the villain.

Consider that each step or "brick" of the Struggle and Relief acts almost as a small story inside of itself. Each of these scenes includes its own problem, and it may even include its own guide, its own paradigm shift, and its own small transformation.

One step of Struggle and Relief could look like this:

- Problem or struggle
- Guide

- Paradigm shift
- Resolution/relief

Here are some simple prompts you can use for each step:

I tried this (it wasn't working) . . .
I realized this (or someone suggested something) . . .
I tried it this new way . . .
This is what happened . . .

You can work on a few of these (shoot for three to five) and then stack them on top of each other to take your reader on a bit of a roller-coaster ride.

No matter what your story is about, here's what I know: I know you struggled to find your way to resolution. I know you found some relief along the way too, or you wouldn't have had the resolve to keep going.

Tell us about it. Every last detail. Take us on the ride of your life.

THE RIDE OF YOUR LIFE

If you took any little slice of your life at all, you'd find struggle and relief. Struggle to climb out of bed but get your coffee. Struggle to get to the office on time but slide in just before nine. Struggle to be productive with everything you have going on but end up having a really fulfilling

THE PATH TO RESOLUTION

day. Struggle to be a good dad but have a sweet moment with your daughter. I love playing with Struggle and Relief because I find it very accurately represents the sweetness (and challenges) of real life.

My family has been on quite the ride in the past couple of years. We've had a lot of exciting developments in our life and some not-so-exciting ones.

1. We got married and pregnant.
2. We went into lockdown during the COVID-19 pandemic.
3. My husband made a massive career change.
4. We welcomed my daughter into the world.
5. The fires in LA pushed us out of the city.
6. We moved across the country.
7. We bought a house.
8. We had a surprise pregnancy.
9. I had an unexpected kidney surgery.

I could go on but I don't need to. The point I want to make is that no matter what slice of life you have chosen to write about, it's bound to be full of ups and downs, Struggle and Relief. No matter what story you're here to tell, there is a list of steps you took along the way that guided you toward your resolution. Resolution didn't come immediately. Each step was needed. Each step taught you something, changed you, or shifted your perspective. Without each of these unique steps, you'd never be here, right where you are.

The list of events I shared above could be just that: a list of events. Or they can be a story. They can be a connected thing, an organism that has a life and a soul and an essence unto itself. Without the framework of a story, the above list is just a set of things that have happened to me. But once it becomes a story, it starts to say something about me as the hero and about the life I'm living. In order for a list of events to become a story, I need . . .

1. To decide what the story is really about (the Controlling Idea)
2. To choose where to enter the story (the Opening Line)
3. To make myself the hero and determine what I want that I don't already have (the Hero Who Wants Something).
4. To name the main obstacle getting in my way (the One Big Problem)
5. To choose a person or handful of people who will help me change (the guide)
6. To use the above list as a path for the hero to follow (the Struggle and Relief)
7. To reach eventual "success," whatever that looks like for your hero (the transformation)
8. To decide what it all means (the moral)

Your life is full of Struggle and Relief. All of our lives are. But what if you were able to see each "loop" on the roller coaster as a stepping stone on the path of who you are becoming?

You've walked a long road to get to where you are. There have been hundreds of steps you've had to take. Maybe some of the steps brought more struggle than relief. This is your opportunity to spell it all out. Every twist, every turn, every disappointment, every failure is important. Each brick holds a lesson for the hero. Each "failure" is part of his transformation. Every small bit of relief keeps her coming back for more.

What a wild ride it is, this life.

CHAPTER 9

Closing the Loops
(The Resolution)

There's a moment in storytelling—right before the resolution—where it seems like the story is in a darker place than ever before. It seems like the hero might not actually change. It appears that all the fight and struggle and sweat equity the hero has put into his own transformation might not actually pay off in the end. There's a sinking feeling that the story ends in failure.

Blake Snyder calls this the All is Lost moment, appropriately so because at this point in the story, it really does feel like all is lost.

As a storytelling device, the All Is Lost moment is incredibly effective because it grips the reader's attention most strongly when the story is nearing an end. Just when you worry the reader might lose attention (because the conflict is about to resolve), she doesn't. In fact, she'll be more engaged than ever because the hero she's been rooting for is about to fall flat on his face.

In addition to heightening the attention of the reader at this point, this device also intensifies the relief that comes in just a minute, when the story *does* finally resolve. Because of the placement of this dark moment in the story, the resolution (which is right around the corner) ends up feeling even *more* valuable to the reader because she sees clearly what could have been lost if this moment never came. The transformation the hero makes will seem even *more* heroic when this literary device is used.

I don't teach the All Is Lost moment as a separate part of the WYS framework because I find it's already kind of wrapped up in the Struggle and Relief Series, and because Synder's Save the Cat model does a great job of teaching it itself. But I mention it here because I find most people who say they are ready to write their story are living in or around their very own All Is Lost moment.

As it relates to personal storytelling, this is a pivotal and absolutely magical moment in the story.

At the point in our personal stories when we are most lost, most afraid, most confused, and most convinced that we will *never* find a resolution to our story—this is when writing your story gives you the most power. You are inches away from an answer to your question. You are on the cusp of your own personal transformation. But it doesn't feel like that. It feels like . . . well . . . like *all is lost*. It's at this point in the story that you have two choices: One is to assume that all *is* in fact lost, and the story ends here. The second is to write toward your resolution.

At the point in our personal stories when we are most lost, most afraid, most confused, and most convinced that we will never find a resolution to our story—this is when writing your story gives you the most power.

The All Is Lost moment is *not* the end of the story. It's inches from the end, and it's the easiest (and most tragic) place to give up. If you don't understand how All Is Lost moments work, you will *think* your story ended in a tragedy when in fact it didn't end at all. It's still being written. You're still working out your resolution.

There are many clichés about All Is Lost moments in real life. We say about these moments that you are "three feet from gold," or that "the night is always darkest before the dawn." I have found these clichés to be largely unhelpful. But what I have found to be extremely helpful—both for myself and for those who have trusted me with their stories—is seeing your life through the lens of storytelling. Understanding what exactly causes a story to resolve. And becoming the kind of narrator (and hero) who can see past the darkest moment in a story and take a narrative all the way to its resolution.

I used to tell writers to "wait until their story is resolved" to write about it. But now I see that would be like waiting until you get home before you drive. It's often writing your story that guides you to your inevitable finish line.

WHAT YOU DON'T KNOW ABOUT RESOLUTION

One way for a story to end is for the hero to get exactly what he or she set out to achieve. The action hero saves the family from the burning building. The woman gets the guy she's been tracking for the whole film. The couple finds each other at the top of the Empire State Building. But the hero getting what he wants doesn't, in itself, make for an interesting ending (in fact, sometimes it can feel too predictable to be very moving).

Personal stories end when the hero transforms. Sometimes this means she does in fact get the job, the guy, the promotion, the baby, the house she was after. But sometimes not. Sometimes after everything she's been through, after every challenge she's faced and every obstacle she's overcome, the idea of finally getting what she wants would feel insignificant or trite. She's not the woman she used to be. She's not the version of herself she was at the beginning of the story. She's not the same person who saw the world in that way.

The hero doesn't always get the physical, tangible thing she was after at the beginning of the story. But to consider the story resolved, there are two things that *do* need to happen:

1. The hero must overcome the OBP.
2. The hero must transform.

Let's talk about these one at a time.

We need to witness a moment in the story where the hero overcomes his or her One Big Problem.

If the OBP in your story is that the hero keeps getting drunk, we need to see her get sober. If the OBP in your story is that the hero suffers from anxiety, the reader is going to expect to see your hero face an anxious situation with poise and confidence. The moment the hero *demonstrates* his or her transformation signals to your reader that something has truly changed. It's not just lip service. Something is different.

Second, in order for the story to resolve, we need to see the hero transform. Frankly, if the hero hasn't transformed, he won't be able to solve his OBP; therefore, these two requirements are wrapped up in one another. But for the purposes of your story, I'd love to have you define how your hero transformed.

The hero used to be _____ but now she is _____.

The hero demonstrates this by _____.

At the beginning of your story, and for most of your journey, you didn't have the wisdom or inner fortitude to solve your problem. You were relying on outside help (your guide) to get by, and you were *still* floundering through each test along the way. But all of that is different now. The

hero has put in some reps. She's done her resistance training. We're not just saying that. We can prove it. The way
you prove it to your reader is by writing a climactic scene.

WRITING YOUR CLIMACTIC SCENE

The moment the hero demonstrates her transformation and
overcomes her One Big Problem, in storytelling terms, is
called a Climactic Scene. It's the moment at the Empire
State Building when Tom Hanks and Meg Ryan finally
meet, the moment the Karate Kid does his crane kick and
wins the tournament. This scene signals to the reader that
the hero doesn't just understand how to change. He has
actually changed. He is a new person.

This is the moment in *Wild* where Cheryl Strayed stands
at the Bridge of the Gods after nearly a year of hiking and
lets it all sink in. Physically, she has journeyed thousands
of miles. But this moment isn't just about completing the
physical journey. It's about the emotional passage that she
has made as well.

> It took me years to be the woman my mother
> raised. It took me 4 years, 7 months and 3 days to
> do it, without her. After I lost myself in the wilder-
> ness of my grief, I found my own way out of the
> woods. And I didn't even know where I was going
> until I got there, on the last day of my hike. Thank
> you, I thought over and over again, for everything

the trail had taught me and everything I couldn't yet know.[7]

Who has the hero become? She's become the woman her mother raised. And how did she do that? By losing herself in the "wilderness" of her grief and learning everything the trail had to teach her.

The climactic scene in *Indestructible* doesn't involve much fanfare. I simply stand on the beach, alone, doing yoga by myself. I am not remarried. I don't have a plan for my future. I don't yet know how it's all going to "work out." (I hadn't met Matt, my now-husband, and I had long given up on having children of my own.) But I am at peace with myself. I might even be the slightest bit happy.

As I stood by the ocean, doing the moves in the only way I knew how, I stated to feel like maybe everything was going to be okay. No matter what came next. And the more I did it—the yoga, the breathing, the standing there all radiant and free in front of the ocean—the more I started to feel lit. I was pretty sure it was happiness.[8]

For your story to "pop" off the page and keep the reader engaged, you need a climactic scene. It doesn't have to be a Hollywood-type climactic scene. There's no need to involve the Empire State Building. But your reader (and your brain) both need to know that this change is permanent and embodied. There's no going back to the way things used to be. You have now taken up residence in a new world, and you have a new and empowered way of being.

There's no going back to the way things used to be. You have now taken up residence in a new world, and you have a new and empowered way of being.

AN UNRESOLVED STORY

Jaclyn wanted to write a story about her long-standing battle with a debilitating autoimmune disease. She had four young children at home and, in fact, she'd received her official diagnosis the same week she found out she was pregnant with her fourth child. The doctors told her that she was unlikely to carry her baby to term and that her quality of life would continue to steadily decline over the next few years.

And yet.

And yet she had previously delivered a happy, healthy baby boy at thirty-seven weeks. She didn't want to take her diagnosis at face value. She prayed that there could be more for her. She woke every day with severe pain in her back and her joints. She struggled with headaches that would take her out for a day at a time. She wondered if she'd ever be able to stand and hold her babies without suffering or if she'd ever physically be able to help her kids learn to ride their bikes.

Her story wasn't resolved.

Jaclyn is the hero of her own story, of course. Her One Big Problem is the illness, and the opening line she wrote included a positive pregnancy test during the week of her diagnosis—a pretty good hook, if you ask me. Her guides were her four kids, who were always pulling her into the present moment, despite how physically painful it often felt for her. Her Struggle and Relief Series involved all the various treatments she had received, some that provided relief and others that cost her a fortune.

And yet she kept fighting and kept believing something could change.

At one point in her story, when Jaclyn was particularly dejected by what the illness had done to her, her body, and her family (the All Is Lost moment), she burst into tears in front of her kids and sank to the ground. Her four-year-old came up to her and put his hand on her back.

"What's wrong, Mommy?"

"I don't know how much longer I can do this," Jaclyn cried to her son as he sat there rubbing her back.

"It's okay, Mommy. We can just sit on the floor and play."

Jaclyn stopped crying and stared at her four-year-old. Was he a genius? She rolled that idea around in her mind for a little bit. *We can just sit on the floor and play. We can just sit on the floor and play. Of course we can.*

That week, Jaclyn quit her job and cashed out her 401k. She decided she was going to "sit on the floor and play" with her kids, which also included things like planning a long-anticipated trip to Disney World, coming to a Write Your Story workshop, and just literally sitting on the floor to play.

She had no idea what was going to happen with this illness, but if it was going to steal her future, it sure as hell wasn't going to steal her present.

When I met Jaclyn, she wasn't 100 percent "healed" of her illness, but she was vibrant and excited and full of life. She was a transformed hero. She spoke with confidence about who she was and what she wanted, and she told me she's found methods to keep her symptoms at bay. I know her story isn't fully over (no personal story ever is), but I love the resolution she wrote for herself.

People often worry that to resolve their story they need to tie everything into a perfect bow. They lament that life "doesn't work like that" and that their story will never be perfectly finished. But what if I told you that no story needs a perfect bow? What a story needs is a resolution to the OBP and a hero who has changed. There may be even *more* resolution coming for you in the future that you haven't accessed yet—there likely is! But what if *some* measure of resolve is available to you right now. It's buried in your own transformation.

PROBLEMS ARE PORTALS

The OBP in your story needs to be resolved in order for your brain (and your reader) to see it as finished. If the problems don't get resolved, the loops stay open and the brain remains engaged. But perhaps there is more than one way for a problem to get resolved.

If Jaclyn's OBP is her illness, the rules of story structure say she needs to "overcome" that problem in order for the story to be resolved. If she ends the story and still has the illness, the reader won't register the loop as closed and will still keep seeking a resolution (so will Jaclyn, and the story will keep her hooked). But what if she decides, while writing this story, that in spite of being a problem, her illness is also a portal to a new way of living?

Sometimes stories are resolved when the hero grows strong enough to *overcome* a problem, and sometime stories are resolved when the hero grows brave enough to surrender *to* a problem.

When I was writing the story of my divorce, I had to decide how I wanted the story to resolve. I was the hero, and the OBP was that my then-husband was living a secret life behind my back. Once I discovered what was going on, I had a decision to make: Was I going to leave him, or was I going to stay and try to work it out?

These decisions are individual, and there's no one right choice. The right choice for me, unequivocally, was to leave the toxic marriage. I spent the entire story becoming the kind of person who could walk away from that controlling dynamic without any regret.

In my Struggle and Relief, I battled with feelings of dread and self-hatred and self-doubt. I froze outside the elevator at my divorce attorney's office, practically fainted when I saw a photo on Instagram of my barely ex-husband in the Bahamas with a new woman, and collapsed with grief when I tried to start dating again.

But eventually, the reader needed to see that I was the kind of woman who could endure this experience and retain my joy.

For some, the hero *overcoming* this problem might look like the emergence of a much kinder, more honest man to save the day. This was a suggestion I got from an editor or two while I was pitching the book to publishers—to wait until I was remarried to publish the story. Some people felt the narrative, as it stood, lacked a satisfying ending.

But honestly, even if I was writing fiction and had total control of the narrative, I find the "new husband" ending to leave little to the imagination. The problem gets solved, but the hero doesn't have to change. Why would the hero evolve if her problem gets erased by somebody else swooping in? Isn't that how I ended up in a toxic situation in the first place?

If the hero is going to overcome the problem, the new husband narrative makes sense. If the hero is going to surrender *to* the problem, she might be transported to a world where her problem isn't such a "problem" anymore.

In other words, what if somewhere between freezing at the attorney's office and nearly passing out from shock at her ex-husband's continued confusing behavior, the hero of this story moves *through* her perceived problem only to discover that her dishonest ex-husband wasn't the problem in the first place? What if she moves into a world where she's not looking to a husband to tell her how to feel—because she already *knows* how she feels about herself?

In *Indestructible*, the OBP could be a dishonest ex-husband, as it seems to be at the beginning of the story. Or it could be an extreme lack of self-confidence, a strange taste for abusive behaviors, a resistance to taking accountability for myself and my contributions, and an unconscious hunger for freedom from my own self-criticism. Since you end a story by solving the OBP, you better be sure you know what the problem truly is.

The way you view your One Big Problem often changes as you move through your story. Maybe your OBP is a massive hill you need to climb, and maybe it is no hill at all. Maybe it's your One Big Opportunity to Change.

Problems can be portals. Sometimes we climb the hill of our problems, and sometimes we stand at the bottom of them and watch as they transform in front of our eyes. Sometimes we get over them, and sometimes we travel right *through* them to a world we don't recognize. Our vision has changed. Clarity has arrived. Things don't mean what we thought they meant.

That's what I call a paradigm shift.

"BUT REAL LIFE DOESN'T RESOLVE THE WAY MOVIES DO"

Writers sometimes get frustrated with the fact that real life doesn't resolve the way the movies do, and I suppose that's fair. Screenplays are fiction. Personal stories are not. But take a minute to consider this: What if movies and "real life" are not all that different? What if the resolution to your story is in your hands, just as the resolution of the movie is in the hands of the screenwriter?

I'm not suggesting that you can always bend physical reality. There are some fixed pieces to your story that you can't alter on a whim. But what if an interesting story doesn't require shifting the details? What if an interesting story simply requires a narrator to pay sharp attention? How might you as the narrator look more deeply at what is already present in the story? What if the unchangeable details could be shaped into a more beautiful conclusion?

Our problems don't magically get fixed because we decide we want them fixed. Fairy godmothers don't come down from heaven and wave their magic wands. Our OBP gets resolved because we *become the type of person* who is capable of resolving it. Nothing changes until we change. And when we change, our lives and our stories open up to us.

You could say "life is hard" or "bad things happen to good people," and you could be right. However we choose to write our story, we are *usually* right. But what if your story is asking you to pay a *different* kind of attention? What if the fixed details of your story are begging to be organized into a more satisfying conclusion?

HOW DO YOU WANT YOUR STORY TO RESOLVE?

Matt came to one of our Write Your Story workshops with a story he knew he needed to write but had no idea how to start. He spent the first part of the weekend reiterating that he wasn't a writer and had no idea what his story was actually about. When we asked him what he *did* know, here's what he said:

- He had lost a lucrative job during the pandemic.
- During that time, while he was scrambling to figure out what to do next, he was presented with an exciting opportunity, which used his skills, piqued his interest, and challenged him beyond what he was used to.
- This opportunity had huge potential upsides, financially and otherwise.
- The problem was that the project didn't immediately support his young family, which was growing at the time.
- Additionally, he found himself impossibly ill-equipped to bring this project to life. He knew he was out of his depth but had no idea how much this

opportunity would stretch his capacity and skill set. He and his business partner had faced multiple failed investors, a dozen financial setbacks, and even an unexpected loss of around $150,000.

- He'd been working on the project for two years with no paycheck and was considering giving up.

You may not see it now (Matt didn't), but the above list are the puzzle pieces of a great story. We spent two days putting those details into the story framework that I'm teaching you in this book, and Matt began to see his life experience through the lens of storytelling. He realized what so many writers realize when they get to this place: he was standing at his All Is Lost moment.

I challenged him to write his resolution.

At first, he wasn't sure what to write. He couldn't see *any* way that this was going to end in his favor. There were too many factors out of his control. He couldn't see past the betrayal and the loss of $150,000. He was in the middle of a lawsuit and had a small but powerful group of people against him. I finally coaxed him to consider how the hero would have to transform in order for the story's questions to get answered.

The OBP Matt had identified was that he had invested three years of his life into a project that was now, essentially, stalled with no funding to move it forward. Since there was no way for him to physically resolve that problem while at the workshop, I gave him a suggestion that I give to any writer who is up against an impossible problem. I suggested he write a handful of fictional resolutions.

If you fictionalize a resolution, please don't publish it and act as if it's true. That's bound to get you into trouble. But fictionalizing resolutions to a personal story is a useful thought experiment. Considering multiple ways the story could end is bound to show you that there is more than one path to resolution.

Matt wrote three fictional endings to the story. All three involved some version of the following paragraph, which I'm sharing with permission:

> The day the project opened was a good day for many reasons. But mostly because, as I cut the tape in front of the community we built, all the pain and setbacks and confusion I felt along the way faded into the background. This wasn't the "hardest thing I'd ever done in my life," as I had been saying for three years. This was the most joyful. What a gift it was to play a small role in bringing this to life.

When Matt wrote his fictional resolution, he realized there was something very *real* about it. It affected him in a visceral way. I know this because I watched it happen. All of us did. The entire group watched Matt go from a guy who was about to give up on a tough project (and nobody would have blamed him for it) to a guy who was infused with excitement and joy. Author and speaker Marianne

Williamson says that miracles are sometimes a shift in circumstances, but much more often they are a shift in perspective. I watched Matt have a miraculous shift in perspective that day.

Miracles are sometimes a shift in circumstances, but much more often they are a shift in perspective.

Writing his story made Matt realize how he as the hero would need to transform in order to bring his story to resolution. He would need to go from being the guy who feels frustrated and blocked when things get difficult to the guy who thinks, "What a joy this is to get to do something I love." From being the guy who thinks, "I'm putting too much stress on my family" to the guy who says, "What a privilege that I get the opportunity to even *try* this. What a chance of a lifetime!"

After the weekend event, the change stuck. I know this because Matt is my husband. Because I'm the one who made him come write his story, in spite of his adamant resistance. Because as much as he swore there wasn't really a story to tell here, I knew that writing his story would be worth it for him and for our family.

And I was *right*.

Suddenly, Matt started having fun doing the same things he'd been doing for months—even the things that used to seem mundane. He began to feel empowered to provide for his family, to create something beautiful for the community, and to feel almost like he was destined to achieve the successful outcome he was after.

We don't get to choose how everything goes in our stories, but we do get to choose how we define our problems and who we become in spite of them. And maybe, just maybe, that's more than enough.

CHAPTER 10

The Reason I'm Telling You This (The Moral)

On the face of it, you know what a moral is. The moral of a story is a simple lesson that can be taken from the events that took place inside the story. But in order to understand why the moral of a story matters so much, there are two things you need to see.

The first thing is that, when a story has a moral, the story is told with purpose. No detail is random. Ever. Every single element of the story serves the moral to make sure that the reader doesn't miss it. "The Boy Who Cried Wolf" is not really about a boy or a wolf. It's about how being dishonest with others puts you in danger of losing their trust.

A moral means a story can be about one thing but is really about something different, on a deeper level. Take a minute to think through what your story might *really* be about. On that deeper level.

The second thing to understand about morals is that *every* story has a moral. Even when the moral isn't stated explicitly in the story, your brain will, without fail, deduce (or concoct?) a moral, even if it happens outside of your awareness. Your brain is *so* concerned with making meaning that it won't rest until it finds the "moral" in every experience.

The next time you watch a movie or listen to a friend tell a story from their weekend, pay attention to what your brain is doing. It's pulling from a catalogue of morals you've heard or created in the past, looking for the right fit:

- Nice guys finish last.
- People are mostly kind and good.
- This kind of stuff *always* happens to me.
- Life isn't fair.
- It never pays to be dishonest.
- You can't trust anyone these days!

Your brain attaches a moral to the story so you can file it away in its appropriate category. Once the moral of the story is defined and the story is filed away, it now acts like a filter for how your brain processes information. Information will come in and go through the filter, and anything that doesn't "fit" gets filtered out. If you've decided the world is an unsafe place and people are always looking to take advantage of you, when you meet someone who is being kind to you, you might assume they have an ulterior motive, and you shut them down.

Our brains do *not* like to be wrong.

When you're driving to work and someone cuts you off in traffic, your brain will either "write" a meaning about that situation, or it will pull up a meaning it has already filed away:

- Men are jerks.
- Nobody pays attention to me.
- Driving is scary.
- Nobody messes with me!
- Hmm . . . he must be in a hurry.

The meaning your brain attaches to the story will impact how you respond to the situation. You may challenge the other driver to a duel of sorts, speeding past him and making rude hand gestures. Or you may just shrug your shoulders and go about your day. Your response will almost always be reflective of the meaning you made.

The meaning your brain attaches to the story will impact how you respond to the situation.

Make no mistake: Not all morals are created equal. Not all of them are helpful or supportive. Not all of them are interesting. Not all of them make very good filters for your life or anyone else's. Not all of them take your story where the hero wants to go. Some morals don't translate between time periods or cultures. Sometimes a moral "works" for a time in your life and then needs to be upgraded. The good news is, you can always write (or rewrite) a new moral, even to a very old story.

THE REASON I'M TELLING
YOU THIS IS BECAUSE . . .

When I was writing the story of my divorce, I would often wonder to myself why all of this was *happening to me*. That language—"happening to me"—is not language I would use anymore to talk about much of anything, but that's definitely what I was wondering at the time. Why is this happening to me?

I could feel the heaviness of the question, even though I couldn't quite explain it back then. It's an obvious question to ask when you're handed the diagnosis or given bad news or uncover a piece of information that changes everything. *Why is this happening to me?* But no matter how I answered the question, I always came up with a moral I didn't love.

The morals I came up with back then were things like, "Men are such jerks" or "No one can be trusted" or "The world is an unsafe place." I could feel those morals bumping around inside my brain and body, but they weren't meanings I wanted to stand by. They weren't messages I wanted to write down. They weren't blueprints I wanted to use to guide the rest of my story.

Remember that when you choose a moral, it becomes a filter for all future experiences in your life. It acts as a blueprint for how your stories are built from here forward. This is not woo-woo, self-help manifestation fluff. It's basic neuroscience. The moral you write to your story (consciously or not) carves a pathway in your brain, and once that pathway is carved, it's very difficult for the neuron to travel any other way.

Wouldn't you rather the moral to your story be something sturdy, something you'd like to build a house on?

So, what I did back then to get my brain off the well-worn "he's such a jerk" track was to change the question I was asking. Instead of, "Why is this happening to me?" I started asking myself, "Why am I telling this to a reader?"

As in, literally, why am I writing this down?

At the end of each little vignette of writing, I would write the words: "The reason I'm telling you this is because . . ." Then I'd picture my imaginary reader and write the next few sentences directly to her. At this point, I had no plans to publish. I'd just imagine sending this story to my sister or one of my close friends and saying to that person, "I wrote this for you—here's why I wanted to tell you this story."

Almost every phrase I wrote after that jumpstart would go something like "I'm telling you this because I want you to know how powerful you are, how remarkable, how incredible . . . I want you to know how this—the thing you hate so much right now, the thing that is nearly killing you—is the *best* thing that has ever happened to you. I want you to know how you dodged a bullet, how you can do literally anything you want, how this is the first day of the rest of your life."

Can you feel how much *lighter* that moral feels than the "men are such jerks" moral I'd come up with before?

I'm convinced (although there's no definitive way to prove this) that the only reason I have the life I have today—a very happy marriage, two happy and healthy children—is because I changed the moral I was writing in that story. If I had continued forward with the "men are jerks" moral after my divorce, I never would have even *noticed* my now-husband, who is one of the kindest, gentlest, most sincere people I know. My brain would have glossed right over him or made up a story about how he must be faking it.

The kinder he was to me, the more I would have dismissed it, thrown it out, pushed it away. This is how neural pathways work. There's no way for you to "write" a story in your life that veers from your morals too much. Your brain cares way too much about staying in its well-worn tracks.

Instead, I *did* meet my husband, and we fell in love. Like any relationship, it's not without its bumps in the road, but even when things don't go the way I hope they will, the pathway in my brain doesn't say, "Men are jerks." It says, "You are powerful . . . you get to make a contribution here . . . this is the first day of the rest of your life."

What might become possible when you write a better moral to your story?

WRITING A BETTER MORAL

Think about this. There are thousands (millions?) of things that happen to you in your life that you wouldn't consider committing to paper. Maybe someone *did* cut you off in traffic this morning, but you completely forgot about it. It's a "nothing" event to you. It fades into the oblivion of the monotonous details of your day.

You wouldn't, I assume, write about what kind of cereal you ate this morning or how you took the garbage out before you went to bed last night. There are very few circumstances in which you'd write about the spam call you got at your desk this morning. You simply silenced it because your phone displayed "potential spam."

But then there are the events you *are* committing to paper. The story that made you pick up this book. The fight you had with your sister. Losing your mom at a young age. The "almost" falling-apart of your marriage. The near-death experience. The birth of your daughter. The adoption of twins. The time you almost married a psychopath. The multi-million-dollar company you somehow built with zero money and even less experience.

These stories are the ones where you're still asking yourself, *How did that happen? What did it all mean?*

What if we used a better question to get at the "why" of our stories? Not, Why did this happen to me? (My answer to this question now is: because it did). But, Why am I writing about this? And why is this important to tell a reader?

Asking this question will not only help you come up with a more *interesting* moral for your reader, but it will also help you come up with a moral that is more constructive for *you*, more generative, and a better use of your creative energy. It will produce a moral that is a good blueprint on which to build your world.

I can't think of anything we need more right now.

So why are you telling your reader what you are telling them? Do you want them to know how loved they are? Do you want them to understand where they came from and what they have been handed? Do you want them to see that they stand on a solid foundation of love? Are you writing because you want to warn them of some kind of danger? To awaken in them a love of travel and adventure? To remind them of how strong they are?

There it is. That's your moral.

Why am I telling you this? Because your moral is yours to write, and because a different moral can create a different future.

DIGGING FOR A DEEPER MORAL

You might find as you write your story that your brain has already written a moral, like mine had—a moral like "men are jerks" or something equivalent.

At one of our Write Your Story workshops, we had a group of people with particularly devastating stories. There are always a couple of heavy stories at these workshops.

Stories of unthinkable abuse or loss. But for some reason, this group of writers had an extra dose of heavy. We had three women in the group who had lost young children (one had buried both of her sons).

This group also contained a woman—I'll call her Erika—who had sat with her young son when he was desperately sick with a rare and deadly disease. There were weeks when she wasn't sure her son would survive the complications of his illness. Many others like him hadn't. In those times of profound uncertainty, Erika told us, it was her faith that kept her afloat. She and her husband prayed and prayed and prayed for a miracle.

Eventually, she told the group, "God saved my son."

When we got to the "moral" part of the framework, Erika told us that the meaning she'd made of her story was that God had allowed her family to suffer like this so that she and her husband's faith would grow. The reason her son had survived, she told us, was because of their obedience and deepened faith.

I challenged Erika to go a little bit deeper. I wasn't saying that the meaning she'd made of her story was wrong. There's no such thing as a "wrong" moral, since you are the only one qualified to make the meaning of your story. I was simply aware of three other women in the room whose stories had not resolved in the same way Erika's had, and I wanted to know on their behalf: Why didn't God save *their* children? Was it because their faith wasn't strong enough?

It was obvious Erika didn't think that was true—she didn't believe that her faith was somehow stronger than the faith of the other women in the room. But the idea of revisiting the moral she'd come up with was deeply unsettling for her. It's unnerving to rewrite a moral once we've already "written" it. Even if that moral isn't serving us anymore.

Writing a new moral opens you up to a new world. And, as fancy or exciting as that sounds, a "new" world is also terrifying because, well, it's new. We know how to operate inside this known world. Our brains already have everything in their tidy containers. We understand the rules and the laws of gravity and how everything works. If you make me rewrite a moral to my story, you make me deconstruct what I already *thought* I knew and start over.

Writing a new moral opens you up to a new world.

Now I have to build something else.

And yet it is precisely this deconstruction and reconstruction that makes human beings the beautiful, expansive, always-evolving species that we are. It's precisely why writing our stories, sharing them with others, and being willing to go back to the beginning and rewrite them again is such a brilliant and difficult and generative task. You might think you know what your story means. But what if there is a bigger meaning available? What if something tragic or unexpected happens that shatters the meaning you thought was so sure?

You have to go back to the beginning. You have to rewrite your meaning. And in order to do that, you'll need to see yourself as the narrator you are. You get to decide what this story is all about. You might not get it perfect the first time or even the hundredth time. Which is why you keep on writing your story again and again and again.

I hear from people every now and then who say it feels trite and reductive to write a moral to your life story. Why would you want to put yourself in a box like that? Life doesn't have one fixed meaning. I can see their point. And yet perhaps this is precisely why writing your story matters so much. How else could we continually construct—and reconstruct—the way we see ourselves inside the world?

What if writing (and rewriting) the moral of the story is the bravest, most expansive thing you can do?

The writing and sharing of stories is a powerful invitation to journey deeper into our lives.

Erika wasn't ready to go back to the drawing board with her moral while at the Write Your Story workshop, and I understand. I'm not in the business of making people do things they aren't ready to do. I don't know if she ever upgraded her moral. But if I had to take a wager, here's what I would bet: she hasn't stopped thinking about it. The writing and sharing of stories is a powerful invitation to journey deeper into our lives. Our stories don't stop knocking until we pay attention.

There is no "right" or "wrong" moral to your story, but maybe there is a bigger moral than you originally considered. Morals are generative. They create a new future. Sometimes you write a moral like "Men can't be trusted" or "My faith saved my son," and then you have another experience or meet another person who makes you realize that moral simply isn't big enough anymore. The moral expands so you can expand. You do that by bravely going back to the drawing board (or in this case, the writing board).

I can't think of anything more courageous or beautiful or constructive than using a tool like writing to grow your awareness, your vision, and your compassion to include more of yourself—and more of others—in the world.

CHAPTER 11

Putting It All Together

Last summer when I was on vacation with my family, we had an unexpected few days of rain to kick off our week together. Anxious for something to do, I went digging through the game closet at our rental and found a thousand-piece jigsaw puzzle, which I then spent the next few days putting together with my husband and brother-in-law.

One night, when I should have been sleeping but instead was trying to get one particularly difficult section of the puzzle completed, I started to think about how putting together a jigsaw puzzle is similar to writing a story. You have the pieces. They're right in front of you. You have a basic framework (the cover of the box, or the framework I taught you in this book). But how do the pieces all work together?

You're always waiting for that familiar "click."

The process can be rather addictive. It pulls you in. You want to make sense of something that feels otherwise random and chaotic. You might even stay awake some nights when you really should be sleeping because you're so desperate to figure out how it all fits. But then there's that triumphant feeling, that endlessly delicious satisfaction, when all the pieces click.

> **You want to make sense of something that feels otherwise random and chaotic.**

If you can access it, this is the energy I'd love for you to bring to your writing. Don't imagine that your life depends on it. Don't give yourself a narrow timeline and force your process to fit inside of it. Let me suggest something that I think you might find quite fulfilling. Imagine you're on vacation and it's raining. Imagine you have a cup of tea or a glass of wine or a slice of cake. Imagine you're sitting with a couple of people you feel safe with. There's a puzzle in front of you. Do this for fun. Just start tinkering with the pieces.

You're going to be here anyway (in your life, on vacation, etc.). Might as well have an interesting and engaging way to pass the time. Let it be an absolutely riveting and satisfactory and fun way to spend your days—figuring out how it all clicks.

WHAT HAPPENED?

If you've followed all of the prompts I've shared with you in this book, you've *outlined* your story but you haven't written it yet. Outlining and writing are two distinctly different tasks. So how do you take an outline and turn it into a story?

One of the great catch-22s of learning to write your story is that now that you've learned this framework, you may need to "forget it" in order to get some writing done. The framework helps with structure of the story. But I find if I focus too much on structure while I'm actually writing, it trips me up. My brain argues with me. I write something and immediately delete it. I write something else but a voice tells me it's dumb. It's like having one foot on the gas and one foot on the brake at the same time.

I meant what I said in the early pages of this book: When you understand this framework and put it to work, it opens a world of possibilities. It helps you make better sense of what is happening around you, what is happening inside you, and what role you play in all of it. You begin to see how pliable our lives actually are, how much agency and creativity we have to shape them and direct them where we want them to go.

We do not have total control over anything. But we have a hell of a lot more control than we tend to think.

And yet in order to get to the place where you can play with your story like a puzzle, you might need to start with just getting it down. You might find it helpful to use the prompts I shared with you throughout this book. Or you may need to start with simply answering the question: *What happened?* It might help to think of yourself like a reporter and take yourself back to the time when the story took place. Pretend you are an unbiased observer. Even though you are most certainly not, it's a helpful exercise.

What took place?

What happened first, second, and third?

Forget everything you know about "good" writing. Forget grammar. Forget structure. Forget the framework I just taught you. You might need to list out your story using bullet points. This part of the process is like dumping the pieces of the story out on the table. Like the pieces of a thousand-piece jigsaw puzzle. We'll get to organizing those pieces later.

Don't be surprised if this step feels chaotic and messy. That's what we're doing here. Moving from chaos to order. The framework will provide order. If it feels messy at first, you're doing it right. If it were clean and tidy, your brain wouldn't be obsessing over it. If the answers were simple, the parts organized, the picture already clear—you wouldn't feel compelled to write the story.

One consideration that might bring you some solace in the midst of the chaos is this: watch for patterns, which will inevitably appear. A person or a theme or a statement, which shows up again and again, is always worth noting. You won't always know what a pattern means, but it is almost always trying to show you something important. As you write and consider more deeply what your story is about, know that patterns are like a breadcrumb trail guiding you out of the woods.

You won't always know what a pattern means, but it is almost always trying to show you something important.

THE EDGE PIECES

When you feel ready, you can start building the borders of your puzzle by using the pieces of this framework I have just taught you. The benefits of this framework are its simplicity, the way it lends itself to personal storytelling, and the fact that you've just invested ten chapters in learning it. I hope this framework proves as useful for you as it has for me.

Take the framework you just learned in this book—including your hook, your One Big Problem, and your guide—and put these eight pieces right next to each other. Think of these as the borders of your puzzle, your edge pieces.

1. **Controlling Idea:** This could be a title and subtitle for your story or a short description.
2. **Opening Line:** This is literally the first line of your story.

3. **Hero Who Wants Something**: This is the introduction of your hero, what he or she wants, and maybe the backstory so we know why it's so important.

4. **One Big Problem**: Why can't the hero have what he or she wants?

5. **The Guide**: The introduction of the person who is going to help the hero overcome his or her OBP.

6. **Struggle and Relief Series**: Take your reader on a roller-coaster ride.

7. **Climactic Scene + Hero Transformation**: Resolve the OBP and show your reader how the hero has changed.

8. **Moral of the Story**: What do you make of this?

As you begin to put your edge pieces together, expect to see your story differently. New insights will come through. You'll have a "breakthrough" in one part of the puzzle, which will open up a loop in another part. Old questions get answered, and new, better questions get asked. The picture becomes clearer and clearer.

You might even find yourself up late one night, hovering over your kitchen table, not because you're worried or anxious but because you feel exhilarated at how your life has begun to speak to you. You feel *determined* to understand how it all fits together. You're finally learning why you felt so pulled to write your story.

You're seeing, for the first time, what the puzzle is trying to show you.

YOU ARE THE NARRATOR

An obvious missing piece in the analogy here is that there is no box cover that shows a picture of what your story is supposed to look like. If you were working on a puzzle, you'd set the box in front of you so you could see an image of what you were working on, and you'd know where you were headed. You'd be working toward that obvious finish. But when it comes to writing your story, there is no box cover. There are no rules about what the finished product needs to look like. You get to make it up.

On the one hand, this is incredibly freeing. You are the creator. You get to decide. You can take this story quite literally wherever you want it to go.

On the other hand, this can be a little bit crippling. A blank page can be overwhelming if you're not used to it—and most of us aren't. We're used to operating off of a program, a picture someone else gave us for our life. We're not used to being told *we* get to decide how it looks, and we're even less prepared to make it up from scratch.

But the fact of the matter is you get to decide how you want your story to read. You're the narrator, the one who sees the ending of the story when it has barely just begun. You don't always get to choose what's on each puzzle piece, but you sure do get to choose how they all fit together. You—and only you—can decide how you want the picture to look.

I have found that the more practice I get with this, the more sophisticated a narrator I become. The more

I write my story, the more I'm able to expertly put the pieces together. The more I'm able to find rest during the times when I get stuck, when things still just don't seem to want to make sense. The more I work with my story, the more I'm able to trust the invisible hand that seems to guide my process.

The longer I lean into this, the more I'm able to trust that no matter how chaotic things seem, the story always finds its way to clarity in the end.

CHAPTER 12

Writing about Those
Who Hurt You

Writers often want to know how they're supposed to write about the more "complicated" characters in their stories—like ex-husbands or abusive parents or shady business partners. On the one hand, I'm of the belief that you only have one choice in the matter: to write the story the way it happened. You can't "sort of" write your story, leaving out the parts that might hurt somebody's feelings. I agree with Anne Lamott when she says that if those people wanted you to write warmly about them, they should have behaved better.

And yet I know that writing the story "the way it happened" is complicated for many reasons, starting with the fact that your memory can be flawed. Memories are notoriously inaccurate. The way it happened in your memory might be different from the way it happened in their memory.

When I first started thinking about publishing *Indestructible*, I worried about the emotional and even physical ramifications I might suffer for telling my side of the story. First of all, I wasn't sure if I was legally allowed to share the details. (Our divorce records had been closed at my ex-husband's request.) And while I wasn't even sure my ex would read whatever I published, what I knew for certain was that he was committed to secrecy. I'd become a good student of his secrecy over the years I'd known him, and the fear of breaking that silence lived in my bones.

When you write your story, you're breaking the fear, as much as or more than you're breaking the silence.

When you write your story, you're breaking the fear, as much as or more than you're breaking the silence.

As a way of reassuring myself (and probably also stalling), I started making phone calls to a few friends who were attorneys of various kinds. They were each practicing in different states with different disciplines, so none of them could "officially" give me legal advice, but each one kindly answered my questions while I took notes. What I noticed in those four phone calls was that, despite getting four different perspectives from four different attorneys, there was one phrase that was repeated four distinct times: *The truth is an absolute defense.*

Essentially what this meant, they explained, was that if my ex-husband did choose to take legal action against me, telling the truth was my best shot at winning in court. After all, it's hard to argue with the truth.

I thought about this endlessly while I edited the story and prepared to share it beyond my group of family and friends. I reminded myself of the legal validity of this statement and also of the spiritual validity. If I could bring myself to tell the truth, the whole truth, and nothing but the truth, I would be free. It was a tall order, but it's what I set out to do.

For me, this meant sharing details that had lived in silence for too long. Things like having a bottle of Gatorade thrown in my face, hiding a miscarriage because I was scared he would be angry if I told him I was sad, or repeated instances of being belittled and shamed for something as simple as trying to speak up at a dinner party. I needed to put these moments down on the page so I could stop carrying them inside my body.

It also meant leaving out certain details, as salacious as they were, because I couldn't remember them very clearly. It meant putting a need for vengeance or even justice aside and sharing only the details that served the reader and the story.

I can honestly say that I shared my truth with no intention to harm, and with no animosity or hate. I changed his name in the manuscript *both* because it legally protected me and because the point wasn't to slander him or tear him down. What good would that do?

Why he did what he did wasn't my story to tell.

The truth—the real truth—was that we'd both gotten lost in a situation neither of us totally understood. It was toxic and unacceptable, and I'm glad I finally got out. I hope he finds his way to healing like I most definitely have. I wish him all the love that I have found in my life. That's the truth, and it's a truth I found while I wrote down the story.

You need to know something. You are allowed to tell your story the way *you* remember it happening. You don't need anyone's permission to do so, but I will give it to you anyway. As you put down the words, you may run into parts where you question your recollection. You might realize you need to ask more questions, to check with bystanders, to go back and look again at details you thought you had nailed down. Writing your story will challenge your definition of "truth," even as it encourages you to be freer to say what you experienced.

You are allowed to tell your story the way you remember it happening.

I'd say that is the writing *doing its job*.

Choosing true words to put on the page is, in my view, not about remembering exact words spoken or naming the specific color of every passing car. You're allowed to omit details if you can't remember them. Sharing true words in a personal story is about accurately representing the personal transformation of the hero.

The more you focus on *that*—your heroic transformation—the less attention other characters get, and the less it all matters anyway. You are the center point. Your truth is not The Truth, but it is *a* truth—and that truth deserves to be here.

When I write about the villains in my story, I always try to remind myself that while villains in stories are fixed devices used to help the hero unfold, actual *people* are not like that. Human beings are dynamic and changing. We are ever-evolving. Even the greatest villain in your personal story has the right to evolve and become someone new. I'm not promising they *will* evolve, but they certainly deserve that opportunity.

Remember, they are a hero in their own story, even though they acted like a villain in yours.

Perhaps you were the villain in someone else's story. You likely have been. How would you like that story to be told? Would you like the author to treat the telling of that story as their golden opportunity to air your dirty laundry and get revenge? Or would you rather they focus on what matters most—how your actions affected *them*?

It's my experience that writing our story helps us fall deeper in love with life itself, *including* the villains who help us change. Writing demystifies the villains in our lives and helps us to see that they were actually vehicles for our own evolution. Abusers ought to be jailed, perpetrators must be held accountable for their actions, and terrorists need to be stopped from inflicting terror. But all of us deserve the right to write our own stories. And even villains deserve the opportunity to change.

WHY A VILLAIN ENTERS A STORY

In order to decide what details to include about the villain in your story and which ones to leave out, it can be helpful to understand *why* villains enter the story in the first place and what purpose they serve as a narrative device. In other words, if you want the details you include about the villain to serve the reader and the story, how do you know which details will do that?

From a narrative perspective, villains enter the story with one purpose and one purpose only: to facilitate and expedite the transformation of the hero. Not every story has a villain, but the ones that do have an added benefit: extra tension, which is useful in building the arc of the story. Remember that the more tension present inside the story, the more quickly and efficiently the hero has the opportunity to change.

The greater the tension, the greater the arc.

So, if there's a villain in your story, congratulations. Consider it an initiation. The villain is here for one reason and one reason only—to serve your evolution. Share all the details about this person that help the reader understand how this frustrating character helped you to evolve. And then focus the narrative more on who you became because of the way you were treated, and less on how the villain acted.

There may be details you need to share that are less than favorable to the villain's reputation. That's fine. You're not here to protect reputations. You're here to write a story. But don't include details for the sake of revenge or even self-proclaimed justice. Those will only weaken the narrative.

The tension villains provide is a great gift if you allow it be. Tension is the X factor that facilitates your growth, the resistance that produces your strength, and the very thing you needed in order to change.

CHAPTER 13

Creating a Writing Ritual

When I first started teaching about writing, I made a big deal out of "having discipline." Ironically, this was during a time in my life when I had no children, no mortgage, and a very flexible job, and when, frankly, I could escape to a "cabin in the woods" whenever I wanted or needed to. I had made my writing the most important thing in my life because, at the time, it *was*. And since I was teaching from my own experience, I'm embarrassed to admit that I imposed that same standard on others.

Imposing one's own standard on others is a problem, because it makes writing appear inaccessible for a whole host of people. Like mothers of young children, or anyone with an unpredictable schedule. Busy executives who can't commit to writing every morning. Folks with disabilities like ADHD who wouldn't be served by sitting still for two hours to write. The list could go on.

Fortunately, I have learned as I've matured that writing doesn't have to be the most important part of your life in order to be a really beautiful part of it. Creating a writing ritual helps you integrate this practice into your days in a way that serves you, the writer. When you focus on ritual over discipline, writing becomes addictive, rather than being another weighty thing on your to-do list that you can't seem to accomplish.

As my life circumstances have evolved, my writing practice has had to evolve too. Now that I have young children, for example, writing first thing in the morning isn't always an option for me the way it used to be. So I've had to keep the spirit of that "discipline," which is really about understanding your brain as a muscle that gets tired throughout the day, and getting some writing done before your brain is out of metaphorical juice. So maybe you don't write first thing every morning. No big deal. But perhaps you write for a few hours one morning per week.

What I've discovered is that *ritual* is much more effective (and fun) than discipline ever was.

The difference between ritual and discipline is subtle but important. Ritual is flexible whereas discipline is rigid. Ritual is invitational whereas discipline is dictatorial. When you create a writing ritual, you get to make it look how *you* want it to look. You're allowed to make it work for you—like *really* work. There are no rules here, but there are some guidelines that can be helpful.

Creating rituals is about having a certain set of things you do (or don't do) before, during, and after you write that make space for the writing to happen. Sometimes you're going to miss a writing session, and that's fine. Sometimes you'll go months without writing—that's also fine. Sometimes you'll have a writing session where not much seems to be happening. Also fine.

These rituals are not about disciplining yourself to "get the words on the page." They're about nurturing the *whole person you are*, knowing that creativity is a natural human response to feeling fully nurtured.

BEFORE YOU WRITE

Everyone is different, and everyone works differently, but using what I have learned about the brain and creativity over the years, I'd love to share a handful of "best practices" I've found that set me up for success before I even sit down to write:

1. **Schedule your writing session ahead of time.** Don't leave to chance whether or not you will write or when you will write. Remove decision fatigue by scheduling the session ahead of time and putting it on the calendar. Treat that writing session the same way you would a doctor's appointment or any other important commitment. You don't cancel unless

you're sick or there is an emergency. This is your sacred time.

2. **See your brain and your body as connected.** When you take care of your body, you take care of your brain. What you eat and drink, how well you sleep, and whether or not you exercise will impact your mental clarity and your ability to write the next day. Keep this in mind and nurture your body to nurture your writing.

3. **Write in the morning if you're able to.** It's not always possible to write first thing in the morning, but if you can, you'll get more done. Your brain is a muscle, and just like any other muscle, it gets tired by the end of the day. (Some writers do get more writing done late at night, after everyone is in bed. If you are one of those people who gets a second creative wind late at night, this strategy could work for you.)

4. **Stay present.** Writing requires presence and honesty and an ability to cut through the noise that's blocking the truth. This is another reason why writing early in the morning (or late at night) can be effective. You have fewer distractions, and you're less likely to be thinking about something else you ought to be doing (you're unlikely to have any meetings scheduled at 5 a.m.).

5. **Get your heart rate up.** One great way to "get present" is to get your heart rate up. I swear by

taking a brisk walk or yoga class before a writing session. When you're feeling blocked or stuck in your writing, try standing up and doing a few jumping jacks by your desk and then sitting down to write again. You might feel a little dumb, but it usually works!

6. **Write to "One Perfect Reader."** Writing is easier if there is a destination for what you are sharing. Imagine composing an email with the subject line "What's been up with me lately," but not knowing who it was going to be sent to. You'd have a really hard time knowing what details to include, what to leave out, and what tone to strike that would best fit the recipient. Is the message going to your child? Your grandparent? Your brother? Your best friend? The destination changes the tone of the content. Before you write your story, decide on *one* perfect reader you would like to read your story when you're done. Maybe it's a therapist. Maybe it's your spouse. Maybe it's a trusted friend. Forget publishing (for now) and focus on that one person you'd like to read your story after it's written.

When you set yourself up for a positive writing session with these simple principles, writing your story can become engaging, interesting, and exciting while also allowing you to have an effortless flow—kind of like putting together a jigsaw puzzle.

WHILE YOU'RE WRITING

People always want to know, "Where should I start?" My answer for this is to start where it's easiest. Usually that's at the beginning of the story, but it might not be for you. Maybe starting a year before the "beginning" of the story is what feels easiest. Later you may decide to delete your first couple of pages and start with what you wrote on page 3. That's fine. Your brain needs to do whatever it takes to get into its creative flow and get the writing done.

For some writers, it's easier to start at the end of the story—or to start with where they are today (which isn't always at the end). If that feels easiest for you, start there. Or start smack-dab in the middle if that's where your brain is trying to go.

While you're writing, don't stop your brain from going where it wants to go.

While you're writing, don't stop your brain from going where it wants to go. What you're looking for is an easy, effortless flow.

Your goal for your writing session should be to just keep moving forward. What you write doesn't have to be perfect (it won't be). It doesn't have to be grammatically correct (it usually isn't). It doesn't even have to have complete sentences. Write bullet points or single words, or start seven different paragraphs you don't finish. Your urge to get it "just right" will get in the way of getting the writing done.

While you're writing, don't think about word count or grammar or deadlines. If you can, put out of your mind the idea of publishing your story. Forget about who might read it, except for your one perfect reader. Just see if you can make a small bit of progress on the story every day. You'll always be able to come back to it and edit tomorrow.

AFTER YOU WRITE

Something I do personally, and I coach my clients to do after they write, is what I call letting the writing rest. This basically means that when you finish writing something, you don't go back and read it a bunch of times. You write it and then move on to the next piece of writing or the next part of the story, and you only come back to what you've written after a period of time to evaluate what needs to change.

The problem with reading and rereading what you've written immediately after writing it is that you won't have very much objectivity about how good or interesting it is. After a few days—or sometimes weeks—you'll be able to open something you wrote and evaluate it honestly. You'll suddenly see that the opening line isn't as interesting as you thought it was to begin with, that the problem isn't physical enough, or that the one offhand line you wrote was quite inspired and beautifully written.

If you edit your own work too quickly, you'll often delete sections that should have been kept or overedit sections that could have been deleted altogether. When you come back to your writing after a period of time, you'll be much better at evaluating it honestly.

The obvious question that follows is: How much time do I wait? The answer varies from writer to writer and project to project. My personal rule of thumb is at least twenty-four hours. I rarely read a piece of writing immediately after I write it (and I regret it if I do). Sometimes, if it serves the writing, I'll read it the following day to set me up for what I'm writing next. For example, if I'm working on a book, I might write Chapter 1 on a Tuesday, let it rest, and then read Chapter 1 on a Wednesday before writing Chapter 2.

But I think waiting even longer than twenty-four hours can be helpful to give yourself the space and objectivity you need. When I finished my first draft of *Indestructible*, I let it rest for over a year before rereading it to consider the possibility of publication.

FALL IN LOVE WITH THE PROCESS

The authors I've worked with over the years who have been the most successful in what they're trying to do are all people who have been willing to embrace an energy of play. Even when it comes to their work, they see it as play.

In other words, can you see the work on your story the same way I saw the work on that jigsaw puzzle while my family was at the beach? Can this be a fun and relaxing and maybe mildly obsessive thing you do to entertain yourself and pass the time? If you're able to do this, you won't believe the gifts and insights that will come through for you. You'll be shocked at what unfolds when you sit down to write your story.

If you're so fixated on getting some specific outcome (like getting on a bestseller list, for example) that you're unable to enjoy the process, you're less likely to keep writing and, therefore, less likely to achieve your objective. All the joy and goodness available in this writing journey comes from the *process*. Not the result. Fall in love with the process, and anything is possible.

Fall in love with the process, and anything is possible.

The energy of play gives you a longevity in your writing that you wouldn't otherwise have. You're not trying to reach "The End." What's the end anyway? What do you do when you finish a puzzle? You mix it up so you can put it together all over again. I pray you never run out of ways to write (and rewrite) your life.

No matter how much sense we make of one thing, there's always something else that doesn't quite add up. Your life is trying to show you something. It's whispering secrets. There's buried wisdom in every single experience if you're willing to dig for it.

The framework isn't everything. It's just a framework.

The formula isn't magic. *You're* the magic.

But sometimes a little ritual can help us build the life and world we want.

CHAPTER 14

Sharing Your Story

When I started taking improv classes, I didn't mean for it to get to this point. When I say "this point," what I mean is that, last night, I performed a show in front of a live audience. What started as an inexplicable impulse to take an intro-level improv class ended last night with me standing in front of a sold-out crowd, saying lines I didn't know I was going to say until they came out of my mouth.

It's one thing to play improv games with a group of friends in a too-hot loft once a week. It's a wholly different experience to stand in the spotlight in front of an expectant audience with no idea what's going to happen next.

The experience made me think of you, since I'm not a beginner anymore at writing or sharing my story but, thanks to improv, I *do* know what it feels like to be a beginner. I wonder if you feel about sharing your story a bit like I felt about standing on that well-lit stage last night: slightly terrified and in over my head.

When you share your story, you're not just sharing your story. You're sharing yourself, your heart, your perspective, your take. You're letting the reader in on things they never would have known if you hadn't shared your story with them—like your hero's inner dialogue or the internal obstacles you faced along the way. Or the meaning you've made of your story, which is ultimately the meaning you're making of your life.

When you share your story, you're not just sharing your story. You're sharing yourself, your heart, your perspective, your take.

Despite how uncomfortable it can be, I'm adamant that sharing your story *has* to be part of the process I'm teaching you. You're not really done writing your story until you share it with someone else.

WHAT DOES IT MEAN TO SHARE YOUR STORY?

When most people hear me talk about "sharing" a story, they assume I mean publishing. But publishing is only one way of sharing a story. You could also share your story with a therapist or with a close friend or relative. You could share your story with your spouse as a way to help them understand you better. You could share your story with your small group at church or with your children or with a handful of friends.

And yes, you could obviously include this story as one of several stories inside a book. If you string together twenty to thirty stories like the one you wrote here, you have something beginning to resemble a memoir.

When I finished writing *Indestructible*, I shared it almost immediately with a group of about ten close friends. These were friends who had watched me live through hell for a handful of years, and I wanted them to know what had really happened. I wanted to tell them the version of the story I'd felt too afraid to share until now. It felt nice, I admit, to come clean on what I'd been going through after so many years of keeping secrets.

Additionally, that group of early readers had each played a pivotal role in helping me to exit my toxic relationship. I hoped that, as they read the story, they would recognize themselves as my guides and be able to see the specific ways they had shifted my perspective throughout the narrative.

But there was another reason I shared my story with my close friends. I wanted to open a dialogue about the story. I wanted to know things like

- Does the story make sense to you?
- Where do you get lost?
- What questions do you still have?
- Does it feel like it's missing anything?

Opening up a dialogue about your story is an optional part of sharing. (You could also say, "I'm not open to feedback right now; I just wanted you to know where I'm coming from.") But for me, posing these questions to a few safe friends helped me get clarity on where my story still needed some development. I was able to take gentle feedback, check in with myself, and edit the story to make it even more clear and resolute.

Sharing my divorce story with a close group of friends gave me the additional perspective I needed to completely close the loop for myself. I assumed that was as far as it would go.

But nearly a year after I finished that story, I started to think about possibly publishing it. I shared the story with two different literary agents, who both told me, separately, that they didn't feel comfortable representing the book for various reasons. I shared it with acquisitions editors at a few publishing houses, who gave me feedback on edits they wanted me to make before they took on the project.

Like I mentioned earlier, one acquisitions editor told me she didn't feel that my story was over yet. She wanted me to wait until I was married again and to use that event as the "resolution" of my story. While I could see where she was coming from, I disagreed with her about how my story was meant to resolve. I wanted the story to resolve with *me* understanding my value and being able to stand on my own two feet.

Sharing your story takes courage and a strong sense of self, knowing that only *you* could know how the story ought to go.

One of the reasons sharing a story can feel challenging is because sharing, in any capacity, opens us up to receiving feedback from other people. Some people might not understand your story. Some might want it told a different way. Some might have valid criticism or even questions ("Why did it take you so long to leave?" "Why didn't you just . . . ?" "Why did you marry that guy in the first place?") And they're entitled to their perspective, no matter how far off it might seem to you.

When Prince Harry's memoir, *Spare*, came out, it lit a firestorm of controversy. It's not the first book to invite complicated conversations, but I felt for Harry (without knowing him personally), since it's a special kind of "complicated" when the controversy is about how you told your story in your own words.

And yet once I read the book, I understood some of the confusion. There were certain aspects of story structure that weren't 100 percent satisfied, in my opinion. My main complaint was that, as a reader, I wasn't totally convinced of the author's transformation by the end of the narrative. I wanted to see Harry realize that he didn't need his family's approval, that he wasn't just some backup to the real deal of his brother. I wanted to see him accept himself fully. And personally, I didn't feel the punch of that resolution by the end of the book.

Of course, that is just my perspective, and my perspective doesn't count for much. At the end of the day, it is Harry's story to tell, and only Harry can decide how he wants to tell it.

We all deserve to tell our stories in the way we choose to tell them. We each deserve to decide when our resolution is complete, even if a literary agent or an acquisitions editor or the general public or some random writing coach doesn't agree with us.

We all deserve to tell our stories in the way we choose to tell them.

I want to remind you that while sharing your story is powerful and important, *publishing* your story is optional. Publishing your story broadens the conversation. It opens you up to feedback from strangers. It takes away the option for you to say, "I'm not open to feedback right now." Suddenly, you're getting feedback you didn't ask for from "Steve" on Amazon.

Publishing is wonderful for a thousand reasons. And yet, as it relates to your personal story, it won't do for you what you think it will. It won't make you feel seen. It might even make you feel *more* misunderstood. If you do choose to publish, I hope you don't lose your own voice along the way. I hope you're able to tell your story in your own way.

Publishing professionals know things you don't know, yes. The public deserves to state their opinion, sure. But you and *only you* know how your story is meant to be told.

As you take the courage to share your story—whatever that looks like for you—know that you'll also be met with perhaps one of the greatest responses in all of human history, the crowning jewel of anyone who chooses to commit themselves to this process: Someone will read what you've written, and they'll say to you, "I saw myself in your story." Or even, "I read your story and it helped me [in some specific way]."

The urge to write your story is the urge to organize and clarify, yes. But I also believe it's an urge to connect. You are not alone in this big, confusing world. You are inextricably tied to others. We are more the same than we are different. Our stories reveal the thread that holds all of us together.

We are more the same than we are different. Our stories reveal the thread that holds all of us together.

SHOULD I PUBLISH THIS?

I know this question may be lingering in the back of your mind: "Should I publish this?" Your answer might be *Absolutely not*. If that's the case, fine. At the Write Your Story workshops, we've had people come with a story they knew they wanted to publish, and other writers who were writing private personal accounts of how they adopted their children, overcame addiction, or recovered from life-altering abuse. Publishing your story doesn't make it more valuable.

However, if you're thinking you might be interested in publication, there are a few ways you can go about this.

1. **Decide if you want to publish this on your own platform or on another one.** Publishing on your own platform (like a social media profile or blog) would be easy from the standpoint that you're the only gatekeeper for that. You could post your story slowly over time, or you could publish it on a blog and share it with whomever you choose. If you want to publish it using another platform (like a magazine or literary journal), that will involve pitching the piece, perfecting it to suit the needs of that publication, and having it be accepted by the editors for publication.

2. **Do you want to keep this story short-form or translate it to long-form?** What I've guided you to do here is to write a story that is three to five pages long. But the principles do translate if you'd like to have this piece evolve into a book or screenplay or some other kind of long-form story. Publication looks different depending on the type of piece you're wanting to publish.

3. **Do you want to write a book?** Book publishing is an involved process, but this framework lends itself

nicely to the manuscript-writing process. In fact, I have an online course called *A Book in Six Months*, which helps you take an idea like the one you've been working on here and turn it into a finished draft in as little as six months. (You can learn more at ABookInSixMonths.com).

Publishing a story is fun and useful for a handful of reasons, but it's not the only way you can share your personal story. You could also

- Share your testimony at a church group or spiritual event
- Pass down your family history to your kids
- Create email content to engage your customers
- Write a speech for your daughter's wedding
- Inspire your employees at the weekly staff meeting
- Give a TED Talk
- Share stories on social media or a blog
- Write a screenplay
- Use the story in therapy

There are so many uses for your story in everyday life. I can't wait to see what you decide to do with the tools you've learned here.

WRITING (AND REWRITING) HISTORY

Most of us learned about history first and foremost through history books. If you went to high school in the US, like I did, this is how you learned about everything from Civil Rights to World Wars I and II to the Great Depression to the Holocaust and Hitler. While there's nothing inherently wrong about learning history from a history book, consider how much inherent bias would be present in a book written by a single person (or small group of people) on any given topic. Even with the utmost care on the part of the author, bias is inevitable—and this doesn't even get at intentional misinformation.

Now think about what would happen if thousands or hundreds of thousands or millions of people contributed their voices to the conversation. What if, fifty years from now, a future generation was learning about something like the COVID-19 pandemic, not by reading a history book but by reading thousands of personal stories from a variety of people who had written about their experiences living through it?

Which education would be more comprehensive?

Which would be truer?

What if there was a book like this—a compilation of stories—about divorce? Adoption? Parenting toddlers? Marriage? Retirement? Menopause?

What if we had this for things like the housing market crash? Or the Kennedy assassination? Stories die with the generation that holds them inside their bodies. Unless we write them down.

It's not that there's no place for books written by a single author covering a specific topic. I work in publishing and have participated in helping dozens of books like that get into print. All of which I'm proud to say have impacted hundreds of thousands or even millions of lives. But the world is made up of eight billion people.

How could one perspective *possibly* be enough?

I have a not-so-secret dream to curate "books" or collections of stories on certain topics like this. In my mind, it wouldn't only be a more equitable and effective way to pass on information to future generations, it would also preserve the kaleidoscope of the human experience.

You write your story for you, yes. But you also write it for me. For us. For our kids and grandkids and on and on. We're writing history together.

Shouldn't your story be part of the conversation?

WRITING PROMPTS

For each chapter's set of questions, use the writing prompts to kick-start your thinking. Use only what you find useful and discard the rest.

Chapter 1
1. What is a story that you've always wanted to tell from your life?
2. What do you guess might happen for you if you give yourself permission to tell your story?
3. Have you written the meaning to your story, or have you taken on the meaning someone else has written for you?
4. Do you think of yourself as an interesting person? Why or why not?
5. What would it look like for you to "share" your story, and why is it important to you?

Chapter 2
1. What is your first reaction to using a framework?
2. Do you find your life boring or interesting? What makes you think of it that way?
3. If your life were speaking to you, what do you think it would be saying?
4. Have you given over the writing of your story to someone else? If so, who?
5. What would it feel like to take back your story and write it for yourself?

Chapter 3
1. What story from your life would you like to write about? If you're having trouble thinking of one, brainstorm a list of five to ten and choose the one with the right amount of charge.
2. Who is your story about? What is he or she like at the beginning of the story?
3. What did the hero overcome?
4. How did the hero change because of the obstacles he or she faced?
5. What might clarity cost you? Is it worth it?

Chapter 4

1. What is a story you feel resistant to telling? You don't have to write it, but often the most interesting, vulnerable, human details are found in the story we least want to tell.
2. What information are you holding back that could unlock your story?
3. Where in your life are you avoiding the things that give a story a hook—tension, upheaval, uncertainty, falling-apart?
4. What is a question you're asking right now, and how could you use that question to shape your story?
5. How can you move past *why* to ask better questions?

Chapter 5

1. Are you the hero or the sidekick in your story? What does it feel like to put yourself at the center of the narrative?
2. If you have resistance to being the hero of a story, what is the resistance about?
3. If stories are built around transformations, how did you transform as the story unfolded?
4. What are some elements of your heroic backstory that might matter to the telling of this story?
5. Who are you at the beginning of the story, and who are you at the end?

Chapter 6

1. What are some problems you're facing in your life as you read this book? List as many as you can think of.
2. Does one problem rise to the surface of the others? Is one more pressing?
3. How does it change the way you think about your problems when you see them as an essential ingredient to your story?
4. How can you take your problems and make them even more tangible for your reader—and for you?
5. If the X factor of growth is problems, how might your problems be helping you to grow?

Chapter 7

1. Who entered your story to help you solve a problem you were facing?
2. How did this person shift your perspective?

3. What progress were you finally able to make thanks to the guide. How did the guide facilitate that progress?
4. What did you think, feel, or do differently at the end of the story that you couldn't think, feel, or do at the beginning?
5. How might your story be shaping you into the guide you hope to become?

Chapter 8
1. Start by listing what happened in your story. What pattern or progress do you see?
2. What are some things you tried along the way that didn't work to resolve your problem?
3. Can you list some moments of "relief" that you experienced along the way?
4. Use both the "struggle" and "relief" to create a Struggle and Relief series based on the lesson in this chapter.
5. What would it feel like to see the roller coaster of your life as a fun game you get to play?

Chapter 9
1. Are you at an "All Is Lost" moment in your story, or can you identify one?
2. If your story hasn't yet been resolved, what would a hopeful resolution look like?
3. How can you, as the hero, demonstrate the transformation that has taken place inside your story?
4. How might the problems you're facing now be a portal to a new world? What is true in that new world?
5. What comes up when you consider your OBP—One Big Opportunity to Change?

Chapter 10
1. Has your brain made up a moral to the story you're telling? How might that moral have been acting like a blueprint for you?
2. Does the moral to your story need an upgrade?
3. What moral(s) would you like to build your life on?
4. How might changing the moral to your story change the way you experience it?
5. What are some past morals you've written that may not fit for your life anymore?

Chapter 11

1. How does it feel to approach writing your story like putting together a jigsaw puzzle?
2. If you are having a hard time with any part of the framework, start by simply writing what happened?
3. What elements of the framework are you most sure about? Can you begin with those?
4. If you are the narrator of your life, how do you want the story to look and sound and feel to your hypothetical reader?
5. If creativity is about moving from chaos to order, what parts of this process feel chaotic to you, and what elements offer more order?

Chapter 12

1. Who is a person you most dread writing about? Why?
2. What are you afraid might happen if you tell the whole story?
3. What would it look like to share the truth from your perspective? Have you given yourself that freedom, even in private?
4. How has the villain in your story helped you fall deeper in love with life itself?
5. In what stories have you been the villain?

Chapter 13

1. What would a life-giving writing ritual look like for you?
2. What time of day would be a good time to write and why?
3. How many days per week can you commit to writing?
4. What are some life habits that would need to shift for you to prioritize writing your story?
5. What would it look like to change your relationship with writing from "have to" to "get to"?

Chapter 14

1. What fears come up for you when you think about sharing your story with one person or a group of people?
2. Who would you most like to share this story with?
3. Have you allowed yourself the freedom to tell your story in your words? If not, what is stopping you?
4. Do you feel called to publish your story? What are some next steps you can take to get there?
5. How does it feel to consider adding your voice to the broader conversation?

ACKNOWLEDGMENTS

A **book might seem** like a solitary accomplishment, but there are dozens of people behind the scenes, without whom you would never be holding this finished product in your hands. I'd like to take a minute to acknowledge some of those people.

First, it needs to be said that I couldn't have written this book without the thousands of clients and friends and participants of the Write Your Story workshops who have vulnerably and graciously shared their stories with me over the years. Thank you for trusting me as a witness and a guide.

I'd like to thank my friend Don Miller for all the ways he has meaningfully contributed to my life and career over the years—including inviting me into the StoryBrand fold, giving me a platform on Business Made Simple, and making many contributions to the content of this book. I'm grateful for your continued friendship and belief in what I have to say.

To my team at Forefront Books—especially my editors (Jill, Amanda, and Janna)—thank you for taking my ideas and helping me clarify them and make them grammatically correct. This is also the first manuscript I've written with toddlers in tow, so thank you for being patient with my constantly moving deadlines. You are publishing pros.

Thank you to all of my mentors and guides, all the ones who have gone before me. Thank you for having the courage to share your words and helping me find the courage to share mine. I am standing on the shoulders of giants.

Thank you, reader, for spending your time and attention and hard-earned money on this book. I made this for you.

And last but *most* certainly not least, thank you to my husband Matt for all the ways you support me and believe in my work even when I don't or can't. You are my best friend, my biggest cheerleader, and the most supportive partner I could have asked for. I love you.

ENDNOTES

1 Andre Agassi, *Open: An Autobiography* (New York: Knopf, 2009), pg. 27.

2 Jennette McCurdy, *I'm Glad My Mom Died* (New York: Simon & Schuster, 2002), pg. 3.

3 Phil Knight, *Shoe Dog: A Memoir by the Creator of Nike* (New York: Scribner, 2016), pg. 9.

4 Laura McKowen, *We Are the Luckiest: The Surprising Magic of a Sober Life* (Novato, CA: New World, 2020), pg. 1.

5 Kendra Cherry, MSEd, "The Zeigarnik Effect and Memory." Verywell Mind, 1 January 2024, https://www.verywell mind.com/zeigarnik-effect-memory-overview-4175150.

6 Start with Blake Snyder's book *Save The Cat! The Last Book on Screenwriting You'll Ever Need*, published in 2005. You may then want to expand into the whole series of Save the Cat books and trainings at SaveTheCat.com.

7 Cheryl Strayed, *Wild: From Lost to Found on the Pacific Crest Trail* (New York: Knopf, 2012), pg. 310.

8 Allison Fallon, *Indestructible: Leveraging Your Broken Heart to Become a Force of Love and Change* (New York: Morgan James, 2019), 158.